If Only God Would Give Me a Sign!

If Only God Would Give Me a Sign!

Linda M. Potter

Word Keepers, Inc.
Published by Bibliocast
Fort Collins, Colorado

Word Keepers, Inc.
Bibliocast/Sat Nam Imprints/Imagine Books/Hawk's Cry Publications

*Books are available at specialty quantity discounts for bulk purchases for
promotions, fund-raising, and educational needs.
For details, write or telephone:*

Word Keepers, Inc.
Tel. 970-225-8058
Fax 877-445-1007
wordkeepersinc@gmail.com
www.wordkeepersinc.com

Cover illustration © 2011 Alece Birnbach
Interior Design: Fleur de Lis DESIGN

Library of Congress Cataloging-in-Publication Data
Potter, Linda M.
If Only God Would Give Me a Sign!/Linda M. Potter
Includes bibliographical references.

ISBN-13: 978-0-9795315-7-6
ISBN-10: 0-9795315-7-8

1. Personal Growth—Humor, life situations 2. Self-Improvement—Creative problem solving through humor, spiritual guidance in everyday signs 3. Inspiration—Heart-warming
family stories of finding spiritual guidance in everyday signs 4. Spirituality—Humor in
awareness of signs all around us 5. Family—Humorous essays 6. Women—Humor

I. Title
First Bibliocast/Word Keepers, Inc. paperback edition May 2011

Printed in the United States of America

10 9 8 7 6 5 4 3 2 1

In loving memory of my mother . . .
Lorraine Marie Hamm

Table of Contents

Epilogue

Yes, that's right, it's the epilogue. I couldn't help myself. Once I got to the end, it screamed to be moved to the front of the book. This ought to give you a good indication of what the rest of the book has in store for you—surprises. Please just read on. I know you'll agree, it just begs to be first.

A while back, a gentleman e-mailed me with a desperate plea for an advance copy of my book. He explained that he was struggling with some life-changing decisions and needed help desperately... NOW! Although he knew the book wasn't yet published, it was *an emergency*, and he needed a sign from God TODAY! He was hoping the book could provide him with the perfect one, the one that was tailor-made for his situation, so he'd gladly pay the printing costs (plus a 20% tip for my time) if I would send a copy of the manuscript directly to his local Kinko's where he could pick it up before 5:00 p.m. that evening. He'd be waiting at the checkout counter since he was sure I'd acquiesce to his emergency.

Strangely enough, this wasn't the first appeal of this type I'd received. One plea came across in some Slavic language that I couldn't decipher, and the Babel Fish translation was even more foreign than the original document. Another request came from a young mother-to-be who wanted to know the sex of her twin babies so she could begin decorating the nursery; and still another, from a small, homeless church community wondering if it was true that "if you build it, they will come."

They all wanted a sign from God to help them find direction and they wanted it right here, right now. Really? Did they think that was how it worked? File a request with the Universe and then sit on the front porch and wait for the UPS guy to "special delivery" your very own ancient scrolls with easy-to-understand answers? I wasn't quite sure how to respond to these queries without sounding inappropriately judgmental.

Finally, I decided to put together a form letter auto-response for such inquiries:

Dear Sir(s) or Madame(s),

"I sincerely appreciate your interest in my book, If Only God Would Give Me a Sign! *Although I don't have a copy to send to you at this time, I do think I can help. Since you appear to need a sign right away, I would be happy to simply loan you one of mine. Considering the nature of your particular challenge (fill in the blank)* _____, *I feel comfortable offering one or more of the following:* **Yield, Help Wanted: Inquire Within,** *or* **Proceed When Clear**. *I have found all three of these to be the best all-purpose ones available, and they work quite well for me when I am faced with important decisions. However, if you are already in crisis mode and need immediate intervention and/or rescuing, you might also want to consider:* **In Case of Flood, Climb to Higher Ground**.

I would add a smiley face, I decided, along with a few words about the importance of maintaining a sense of humor, and a suggestion that s/he or they might want to consider contacting a professional counselor, calling Dial-a-Prayer, or phoning in to a radio talk show hosted by someone like Dr. Frasier Crane, the all-knowing psychiatrist on *Cheers*.

What I wasn't going to try to explain in 200 words or less was that getting a sign 'from God' is actually pretty easy. Recognizing the sign when it plants itself in your path takes a little more skill, and having the courage to follow the guidance you're given ... well, that's a graduate level course where spiritual growth (and the real work) begins.

There are a lot of things this book is *not* and lots of people have pointed that out to me, some with less tact than others. The first agent I contacted about my manuscript sent back a cryptic message which said, in essence, that he really didn't care about my personal spiritual evolution, or the stupid human tricks I'd been performing on the Cosmic stage. He just wanted something he could *sell*—a book that outlined the five (or maybe even as many as ten) steps to getting a no-nonsense, easy-to-interpret sign from God 'on demand.' And if we could package it with a pocket-sized GPS (replace global with 'God') that made sure we *never* lost our way, that would be even better.

I don't have a 1-800 psychic hotline number; I haven't been gifted with any secret formula for getting an undeniably 'authentic' sign from God (like the parting of the Red Sea or some variety of Burning Bush, etc.); and I definitely don't have the answer key to our multiple choice quizzes. If there's some magic ritual involving candles, chanting, and joyful dancing that can get us *what* we want *when* we want it, no one's told me about it. But I do have a few dozen boxes of candles, and I do like chanting and dancing, so maybe I'll see what I can come up with.

What I do know is that signs are everywhere if we're willing to take the time to pay attention. They aren't always metal/plastic/neon/cardboard/paper signs, either. Because we are a hard-copy sign culture—we love our store signs, traffic signs, building signs, billboard signs, bumper stickers, signs on vehicles, signs hanging over the highway, and random signs posted in random places (some even flashing at us), etc.—we're faced with lots of easy-access input virtually every moment of every day. Spirit meets us wherever we're at and posted signs are as convenient a mode of communication as any. But good old-fashioned serendipity is still an excellent way to get signs as well. Show up and pay attention. That's most of it.

The truth is: signs *are* everywhere. What we really want to know is how to recognize the signs when they show up and how to discern, "Which signs are meant for *me*?" If you're paying attention *and* are willing to trust your inner knowing, intuition will lead you to the sign that's "got your name on it." For example, mothers just know which baby is theirs in a hospital nursery filled with newborns. The little wrist tags on the infants are just there for the doctors, the nurses, and the dads. Signs are like that too. You'll just *know* which sign is yours as long as you're willing to keep your heart and your eyes open.

We miss a lot of signs because they aren't what we want to see or hear. Signs get your attention. The rest is up to you. There are several good 'tests' for whether something is or is not a sign. I find the following examples particularly helpful (Feel free to substitute some*one* for some*thing* and vice versa):

- If something grabs your attention ... it's a sign.
- If something sends you into fits of laughter ... it's a sign.
- If something just gives you fits (of any kind) ... it's a sign.
- If something pushes all your buttons ... it's a sign.
- If something elicits any strong emotional reaction ranging from rapture to rage, from fight to flight ... it's a sign.
- If you're told to be/do something that might make you a better person in the long run (especially in spite of yourself) ... it's a sign.
- If you wake up in the middle of the night thinking about a particular thing ... it's a sign.
- If you have the same dream (or some variation of that same theme) repeatedly, whether it's three times or three hundred times ... it's a sign.
- If a book you've never heard of is given to you by three unrelated people as a Christmas gift ... it's a sign.
- If any book falls off the bookstore shelf, smashes your big toe, and opens 'magically' to the page with the message you need to read ... it's an *urgent* sign.
- If someone shows up in your life repeatedly (good *or* bad) ... it's a sign.

- If *anything* shows up in your life repeatedly, particularly within a short period of time ... it's a sign.
- If *I'll Be There* comes on the radio while you're mourning a recent breakup ... it's a sign.
- If a charismatic hottie with Hollywood good looks drives up in a red Ferrari, radiating unconditional love, spouting the consciousness of a Buddha, and magically shows up at your front door with a deluxe gift basket filled with dark chocolates ... it's a miracle, not a sign. (It's important to recognize the difference.)

Every moment of every day, we are inundated with messages from cosmic management: a familiar song on the radio, a déjà vu scenario, a serendipitous meeting with a friend who reveals a great job for you, an *Open* sign in a store window, an annoying *Detour* that takes you a mile out of your way, and so on. But without a chorus of angels, a trumpeting brass section, or bolts of lightning, these ordinary, everyday signs can go unnoticed (by you). And whatever persistent, prompting, prodding visual aid was given is lost.

I lived my life waiting for signs, even for the writing of this book. Waiting ... for a sign ... gave me permission ... to wait for a sign ... to step out of my velvet rut. Waiting for a sign was easy because it required absolutely nothing of me. I could hold out for an eternity if necessary. If that Higher Power wasn't in any hurry to show me a sign ... I wasn't in any hurry to acknowledge one. I became a pro at waiting for guidance.

No matter how big, bold, or in-your-face signs are, we don't recognize them until we're ready to receive them. Was that *Check Baggage* sign at the airport (which triggered an hour's worth of serial giggling) a sign? And how about the *Claim Baggage Here* sign I encountered at my destination, which caused me to tear up a little between sighs of "Do I have to?"

It's a sign of unfolding awareness when we begin to notice signs, partly because we've set our *intention* (to learn and to grow), but also partly because we're paying more *attention*. Our awareness grows and tips the scales toward expanded consciousness. The bonus is that the more open we are, the more signs we experience.

A sign *means* whatever we think it does. Signs are like those Rorschach ink blot tests—they mean something unique to everyone who observes them. The only difference is that there isn't a therapist furiously making notes while you're scrunching up your nose and examining the sign from several different angles.

However, the message a sign holds for us may change as we change. What encountering a *Yield* sign evoked in me as a sixteen-year-old is different than what it triggers for me now. Which interpretation is correct? It's always the one that most completely supports and empowers us *at that moment in time*. The nudge to find a sign is actually coming from our inner spiritual essence longing to be heard. It's that essence that encourages us. It's that inner voice that tells us which sign to pay attention to, which one we most need now.

Signs don't, however, predict the future or determine our fate—they aren't meant to be crystal balls, and even if Bruce Springsteen had put Madame Marie on retainer, she wouldn't have been able to provide any information he couldn't already access himself.

Signs don't provide answers; they challenge us to ask questions. Signs don't tell us where to go; they invite us to look at where we are and begin to ask how to *get* to where we want to go. The signs I've chosen for this book are the ones that have had (and are still having) the most impact on my own personal growth, but they also just happen to reflect possible building blocks of spiritual growth.

Openness, clarity, surrender, release, courage, patience, focus, love, faith, non-judgment, abundance, peace … all the major lessons of the human experience are explored through these signs. Ultimately, all signs point us in the same direction—the one that heads upward, inviting us to higher consciousness.

Writing any book involves a steep learning curve. This book was my leap off into the abyss, from the mountain top onto a Black Diamond ski slope. Okay, I don't ski, but I like colorful metaphors. But, without a doubt, birthing this book had some powerfully moving moments that kept me upright on my "skis" even when the end of the run was nowhere in sight. This was one of them:

I was in the hot tub one night thinking about the book when I had a sudden flash of insight about one of the chapters.

I leaped out of the tub, dashed inside the house, and headed to the den, leaving a trail of dripping water through four rooms of the house before I reached the desk where my laptop was parked.

I flung open the lid and typed frantically for twenty minutes, recording every thought that was pouring in before it could be lost. Exhausted, I finally sat back and stared proudly at the five page document I had just created. I leaned forward to save my work, but before I had a chance to touch the keypad, the entire screen went blank and the computer crashed before my very eyes. As I saw the little 'on' light go dark, my heart stuck in my throat. Shocked, then angry, I yelled, "So what kind of a sign is this?"

At that very moment the computer somehow came back to life, the 'on' button flashed green, and the entire document 'magically' reappeared on the screen. As I raised my hands to my face in both relief and disbelief, I noticed the charm bracelet dangling from my left wrist—the one I'd forgotten to take off before entering the hot tub for my evening soak. As I looked at it more closely, I smiled—the silver bracelet I'd worn for years, but had rarely actually examined, had six dangling hearts surrounding one inscribed disc that read, 'Faith.'

Getting a sign from God is as easy or as difficult as we want it to be. We can spend years asking for signs or a lifetime expressing gratitude for the ones we have been aware enough to notice. Whatever sign you're needing to see right now, I hope it leaps off the page at you and you say, "There it is! That's the sign I've been waiting for."

Remember, the signs are everywhere. Enjoy your journey. No worries, the signs will guide you along, all the way home.

Introduction

I opened my spiral-bound journal with the Victorian tableau on the tea-stained cover, took out my passion pink plumed pen, and began to write feverishly . . .

"It was a dark and stormy night. Really dark, really stormy . . ." So dark I couldn't find the 'on' switch on the emergency flashlight I kept in the kitchen drawer; so dark I didn't realize I'd actually grabbed the digital meat thermometer which was never going to light up anything except a pork roast. And so stormy, I half expected Boris Karloff to peer in through my front living room window, his recycled Frankenstein eyeballs scanning me from head to toe as he contemplated taking me as his bride.

Yes, *that dark and stormy night . . .* The relentless, pounding rain all but obliterated my view of the scenic gravel-pit-turned-lake behind my house, which, by this time, was overflowing its rocky shores, swallowing up the paddleboat I had purchased from Sam's Club the previous summer. I had seen the threatening weather report earlier in the evening, the one that foreshadowed the arrival of the Four Horsemen of the Apocalypse, but I had ignored its dire warning of violent storms and flash floods.

Upon a second thought, I became confused and hysterical, running out onto my deck, falling to my knees, pleading for guidance, and imploring to the dark heavens: *If Only God Would Give Me a Sign!* Suddenly, miraculously, there it was, written in a golden Franklin Gothic font, emblazoned across the sky for a few brief seconds in a brilliant flash of lightning: **In Case of Flood, Climb to Higher Ground**! Then, just as suddenly as it had appeared, it was gone!

"Wait," I cried as I rose to my feet and ran a little too hard toward the deck's edge, bouncing me off the white polyurethane railing as my panicked thoughts raced on. Higher ground? How high is high? Will the hill across the street that leads up to the out-of-my-price-range custom homes be high enough? Do I need to keep climbing beyond that? Should I borrow my neighbor's rowboat?

I always thought it would have been a thrilling, heart-pounding story worthy of a mini-series if it *had* happened like that, if *the* life-changing sign from God that put me on the miracle-laden path to enlightenment had arrived with all the over-the-top, bolts of lightning ripping through the *dark and stormy night sky* in a scene from a Gothic novel. However, spiritual growth defies scripting (no matter how hard I try), and a whole lot of Divine comedy emphatically ends up being infused into my storyline. Instead, my messages from God show up when I least expect them, in places I would never think to look, in ways that I couldn't possibly predict. Go figure.

My *real* breakthrough actually came on an afternoon that was partly cloudy, with a slight chance of rain. Other than throwing myself on my desk, pleading with the patron saint of organization to rescue me from the chaos I laughingly called my office, nothing very dramatic was going on at all. I wasn't experiencing a dark night of the soul. I wasn't facing any life-and-death decisions. I wasn't at the end of my twisted rope, nor was I feeling particularly desperate . . . yet.

I *was* stressed, exhausted, and bemoaning the mediocrity that was *my life*. My story wasn't playing out the way I had expected it to unfold so many years ago. Where, for example, was the lifestyle of the rich and famous I was so sure was my destiny? I would have settled for financially comfortable, moderately successful, and fat and happy. But all I ended up with was 'fat' and it did *not* make me happy. Middle age had come and gone and I had little to show for all those years of toil and trouble. I was over the hill, free falling down the other side, battered and bludgeoned by every rock, tree stump, and gnarly root imbedded in the weed-infested ground on the not-so-sunny side of the street.

That got me to thinking . . . maybe I should do something proactive *before* that dark and stormy night scenario actually becomes a reality; *before* I get hopelessly lost once again in the lightless, overgrown forest of doubt and desperation, only to be rescued by a box of Double Stuf Oreos®. My plan: confront my higher power and *demand* (yeah that would work!) the life I knew I deserved.

Okay, it was an uncharacteristically *bold move* for me. My habitual life pattern was to exhaust every conceivable option before I turned to God for help. I would suffer in silence (more like low-volume whining) until my problem became big enough to warrant divine attention. Yes! Bigger is better! Once that thought congealed, a minor course correction was no longer an option. I needed a full-blown intervention—I begged for a miracle—a commercial grade miracle that would help me claw my way out of the deep, dark hole I now occupied, the one I had once again dug for myself.

Surely, there was some way to break the painful crash-and-burn cycle I had adopted as my life's tool for being in the world. I wanted, no, I *needed* a better life than the one I was experiencing—one, not necessarily *Happy Every After*, but a life of some reasonable balance.

So . . . one perfectly ordinary afternoon, I tossed back a mug of cowboy black coffee. It gave me a false sense of courage, but courage was courage. I pushed through my bedroom French doors. Boldly stepping within inches of the railing at the far end of the deck, I took a nanosecond to survey the landscape to see if anyone was within earshot, and raised my right clenched fist to the heavens: "God, just give me *a sign*! Now!" With my arm still raised, a blurred movement in my husband's garden caught my attention. Two bunnies nibbling the Bibb lettuce patch abruptly stopped eating, their ears on high alert. I lowered my voice and added, "Any sign will do—just something that steers me in the right direction so I can manifest the life I *really* want before I'm too old to enjoy it." Okay, I thought, I'm good to go. I felt a tad ridiculous so I stepped back inside the privacy of my bedroom, collapsed into the recliner, popped up the footrest, and paged through the latest issue of *O Magazine* while I waited for *the sign*.

While I was not exactly sure what I expected to happen, I prepared for anything. Although I knew it was unlikely that blazing stone tablets, with or without Charlton Heston, would magically appear in my front yard, I was still hoping to be wowed. Wowed never showed up. No sign appeared, spectacular or otherwise. After about an hour of reciting in my head all the reasons why my life sucked, I decided to give up on the sign thing and get back to cleaning the oven. Downhearted, I resigned myself to a future without a *deus ex machina* to save the day (the ancient Greek theatre version of dial-a-deity) anywhere in my storyline. That's undoubtedly why, at first, I missed the sign I was sent. It appeared a few days after my dramatic plea. I had already relegated the incident to my "What was I thinking?" file.

So, I certainly wasn't expecting any signs from God that day. It had been a particularly long and exasperating Monday, and all I wanted to do was get home as quickly as possible so I could lock myself in the bedroom with the TV remote and a five-gallon tub of Weight Watchers® ice cream. I should have suspected something was up when I suddenly felt a strong urge to take a quick, unplanned detour to my favorite little bookstore. As I hurried into the shop, I actually passed right by *my sign* without as much as a glance in its direction. As I was exiting the store, destiny intervened. In a senior moment of the "darn it, I can't believe I did that again" kind, I realized I'd left my car keys on the checkout counter. As I spun around and headed back towards the front door, I saw it! The sign—extraordinarily ordinary—stopped me in my tracks.

It wasn't bathed in white light; it didn't burst into flames at my very glance; and it didn't speak to me (at least not literally). Confused and not exactly quite sure *why* I was suddenly so intrigued with an unremarkable white plastic sign, I read its simple message: *Help Wanted.* I'd certainly seen *Help Wanted* signs before. After all, I'd had a store myself, and that familiar red and white sign had appeared in my shop's window many times during the twenty-three years I'd owned the business. Yet, for some reason, this common, no-frills sign was suddenly the most interesting thing on the planet to me. I must have stood there and stared at it for at least fifteen minutes before I finally realized that I'd attracted the attention of two small children, a Cocker Spaniel, and the shop owner who was now standing next to me with a look of deep concern on his face. I let out an awkward laugh, made some nonsensical comment about the unemployment rate, and quickly retreated to my car.

For the next couple of days I couldn't stop thinking about the *Help Wanted* sign. Questions kept popping into my head. Did they just post the sign? What kind of help did they need? Was good help hard to find? Did I need a part-time job?

As I went about my week, I found myself checking the front windows of every store I passed looking for more signs like the one at the bookstore. I discovered six *Help Wanted* signs at the mall, some much larger and more desperate than others. The gas station a mile from my house was looking for help *every* shift; the movie theatre needed a weekday person old enough to view the R-rated films; and my favorite guilty-pleasure fast food restaurant had a permanent *Help Wanted* notice the size of a billboard, adjacent to the front counter.

For the next two weeks, I became obsessed with locating and analyzing, even photographing, every **Help Wanted** sign I could find. Had I lost my mind, or my grasp on reality? Was this God's idea of a practical joke? Maybe I had been so eager to get any sign that I claimed the first one that showed up. Surely, this sudden, overwhelming fascination with **Help Wanted** signs couldn't be merely a coincidence, could it? There had to be a hidden message somewhere. I even considered the possibility that it was in some kind of code. After rearranging the letters in **Help Wanted** at least a dozen times, the only messages I could come up with were "Paw held net" and "Pawn the LED" at which point I realized I was definitely on the wrong track.

Determined to find an answer, I channeled my best Agatha Christie and returned to the bookstore where I'd first noticed my "sign from God"—although by now I was seriously doubting its authenticity—hoping for a life-changing "aha moment" or, at the very least, some further clues. Then I saw something I simply hadn't noticed before.

How could I have missed it? Unlike the other signs, this one said more than **Help Wanted**. Beneath those two familiar words, printed in bold, bright letters several inches high, there was a second line in handwritten script so small, I had to shift my eyeglasses a little higher onto my nose and peer through my seamless bifocals to make it out: *Inquire Within.*

I was looking for a sign from God, a message that would put an end to my struggles and clearly illuminate my spiritual path—and there it was, right in front of me. *Help wanted?* It questioned loudly. Then, by way of an answer, it whispered: *Inquire Within.*

Was this the guidance I'd asked for that crazy afternoon when I demanded a sign from God? Instead of looking outside of myself for solutions as I had in the past, was I being counseled to turn inward? Had I been so busy creating and recreating so much noise in my life that I'd failed to hear the still, small voice within?

Apparently, I was on to something. Over the next few days I began to actually hear the messages that were being delivered day and night. Halfway through my morning banana chocolate chip muffin I found myself grabbing the *TV Guide* and scribbling furiously in the margins. Standing in line at the post office, I was jotting down notes on the back of a customs declaration form. In the middle of the night, sleepwalking my way to the kitchen for a leftover piece of angel food cake with fluffy white icing, I'd be inexplicably diverted to the den where I'd grab a handful of paper out of the printer tray and write until dawn. Evidence of manic downloads were everywhere—sticky notes posted on the bathroom walls, defaced magazine covers laid out on the couch, and ink-smeared napkins stacked under a saltshaker in the kitchen.

Two weeks and eighteen pages of scrawled notes later, I realized that divine guidance isn't about *getting* a sign; it's about becoming aware of signs all around us, guiding us. Signs, the presence of unseen guidance, and intuition were constantly descending through grace all the time.

The more stubborn we are, the more physical the sign's gotta be. *Help Wanted: Inquire Within*—a physical sign that appeared in my path at the exact moment I needed its particular wisdom— **Going *within* for divine guidance assures us that we will never have to go *without*.**

The *Help Wanted* sign was only the beginning. Soon, I began to notice other signs ... *many* other signs. They were everywhere: in store windows, on street corners, along the highways, on my neighbor's chain link fence, on the inside of my grocery sack, on the side of trucks, on the door to my husband's padlocked, private retreat above the garage, and so on. Some made me think: *Open for Business, Detour,* and *No Shirt, No Shoes, No Service.* Some brought me to tears: *Hazardous Conditions May Exist, Slow: Children at Play.* Some made me laugh out loud: *Beware of Dog, Please Do Not Open Packages, Caution: Low Flying Aircraft.* And that made me think of the song, *Signs* © 1970, 2002. (Sign, sign, everywhere a sign ... by the Five Man Electrical Band.)

I recorded every single sign—it became my new favorite obsession—until I finally reined things in after a close encounter of the vehicular kind with a *STOP* sign that ended up in my path as I slid to a halt on an icy road one winter morning.

With all these signs competing for my attention, each with an oddly personal message that seemed somehow custom-selected just for me, I finally had an epiphany: my life was in dire need of an extreme makeover. I took it slowly. I learned that *Fog Conditions May Exist* and to only *Proceed When Clear*. I knew to be cognizant of the *Speed Limit Ahead*, and *Yield* to oncoming traffic. I also learned that all good things are *Free to a Good Home*. My sign awareness has ushered in a few changes in my daily routine. For example, I read, with great interest, the fine print on signs posted in every store, gas station, coffee shop, movie theatre, dentist office, fitness center, lawyer's office, and public restroom; and yes, people stare.

I can now also recite, in order, the messages on every traffic sign between my house and the outlet mall, and I get strangely excited when I encounter a sign I haven't seen before. My expanded awareness has influenced every area of my life. I now notice more of *everything* than I ever have before. For instance, I observed that we have four bald eagles living within a half mile of our home; there are twelve houses in our neighborhood with red doors; and eighty percent of the people living on our block drive silver (or gunmetal gray) SUVs. Interesting. Who knows what else is out there for me to discover along my path? What I do know: the signs are everywhere helping me get where I need to be, every step along my journey.

Open for Business

My relationship with God can best be described as a two-sided plastic sign with *Open* on one side and *Closed* on the other. When it's convenient for me (let's say between the hours of 9–10 p.m.), I'm open to spiritual guidance. At least that's true for most weeks, unless I'm really busy trying to catch up on past episodes of *Glee*. Okay, let's be honest. There have been periods when I've forgotten to flip over that *Closed* sign for weeks at a time. Yet I lament, "My life sucks and I've lost my way. If God would only give me a sign. . . ." It's time to get real. I can't pour holy water into a vessel with a vacuum-sealed lid!

Spirit is trying to contact me every moment of every day with the guidance I am longing for—I simply need to pay attention, turn my sign over to *Open*, schedule in a little God time, and be prepared for everything in my life to change. And, if I'm willing to keep the *Open* sign out permanently, I'll begin to notice guidance everywhere I turn.

A familiar song on the radio that opens my heart, a seemingly random encounter that leads to a job offer, a surprise phone call that rekindles a friendship, a can of creamed corn that falls off a pantry shelf and reminds me that flip flops are no substitute for steel-toed shoes—are all aha *moments* in the making. Note to self: Don't underestimate God's sense of humor.

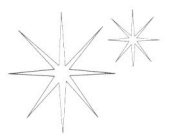
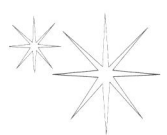

CHAPTER

1

When I was eight years old, I would have sold one of my little brothers for a couple boxes of salty, nutty, crunchy pumpkin seeds. They were my passion. So, it's no surprise that my favorite place in the whole world was the small candy shop across the street from Reinberg Elementary School. Every day, after classes, my friends and I would hurry over to the little store to make our day's purchases. For me, it was usually the pumpkin seeds, but I occasionally opted for a strip of multi-colored candy buttons. For my best friend, Linda B., it was those sticky miniature wax bottles filled with fruit-flavored sugar syrup or a package of Necco Wafers®.

It really didn't matter what we bought. There was just something magical about that little store, and we delighted in every mouth-watering moment spent wandering up and down the crowded aisles.

After school, we would race each other to the end of the playground and gather at the corner across the street from the candy store. From that vantage point, we could just barely see the worn and somewhat crooked *Open* sign that always hung in the front window. That tattered old plaque triggered visions of sugarplums dancing in our heads, and it became a race into the crosswalk as soon as the signal turned green. It never occurred to me that the small store was ever anything but open.

It was a cool, appropriately gloomy, Sunday afternoon when I first learned otherwise. I wasn't supposed to be that far from home. The shop was on a traffic-packed street, and on weekends, there were no crossing guards. I had coaxed my younger brother—whom I wouldn't *really* have pawned for more pumpkin seeds—into the red wagon with promises of licorice snaps and SloPoke® suckers. With Wally in tow, I began the six-block journey to my own special candy land.

Since Wally was starting kindergarten in the fall, and surely joining me and my friends in our daily pilgrimage to the little shop of tasty treasures, I was eager to offer him a tantalizing preview of sweet things to come. As we turned onto the corner where the shop stood, happy anticipation quickly turned to all-out panic. The store was dark. No one was shopping. No one was standing behind the gold cash register. No candies sat in the window calling out like sirens to passing school children. The crooked old sign that always hung in the window was still there, but today it bore a new, incomprehensible message. It said, *Closed.*

Closed? What? How could that be? I pressed my hands up against the glass in the front window and peered inside. I could see the nearly endless row of candy-filled glass bins lined up along the far wall, stretching off into what surely had to be infinity. The teetering tower of Bazooka® Bubble Gum boxes were all still stacked on the counter. The ruby red wax lips in the apothecary jar were smiling back at me with clueless grins, unaware that there was anything wrong. The candy was there, but I couldn't get to it. That *Closed* sign stood between me and everything I wanted.

That may have been my first close encounter with a *Closed* sign, but it wasn't my last. *Closed* signs have showed up on an annoyingly regular basis in my life. Sometimes the loss seemed particularly personal: the neighborhood movie theatre, where I was first traumatized by *The Blob*, shutting its doors; the dance studio, where I tapped my way through grammar school, closing; and the diner, where they still served banana splits in real glass dishes, going out of business. Other times, there wasn't an actual *Closed* sign or even an actual "door," but the message was the same: the perfect job that was too good to be true turned out to be just that; the house of my dreams manifested in someone else's reality; and the relationship that was supposed to last 'til death do us part' took its last breath long before the demise of the two parties involved.

The list goes on. Regardless of the circumstances, it never felt good to be locked out from what I desired.

As the years passed, life often felt like an endless succession of doors that closed just as I approached them, taunting me with thwarted hopes and unrealized expectations (realistic or otherwise). How could I ever have what I wanted if the doors wouldn't open for me—literally *or* figuratively—when I wanted them to? Even worse, how could I live out my dreams when doors that were once open, slammed shut, seemingly without warning?

In my mid-thirties, I decided to open my own small store. We didn't sell candy, but we did offer dolls, teddy bears, and other must-have collectibles. I wanted the store to have a sweet, kid-in-a-candy-store appeal where everything was delectably desirable. In preparation for our grand opening, I completely transformed a dreary gray-walled retail space into a lusciously inviting shop that, in retrospect, looked a little like Munchkinland. I stocked the shelves, arranged the checkout counter, selected the exterior signage, and hired the employees, all with ease. The one thing I kept putting off, though, was purchasing an *Open/Closed* sign.

I knew from my candy store experience that I didn't want to limit anyone's access to the treasures I had to offer, but did that mean I needed to keep the shop open twenty-four hours a day? Somehow, that didn't seem reasonable. I'd barely survived several years of sleep deprivation that came with having three children in less than six years. Staying open all the time would put yet another monumental drain on my ever-dwindling time and energy. Wouldn't setting "impossible" hours be tantamount to hanging a *Closed* sign on the door to my own happiness?

I once knew a local business owner who unabashedly named her store "Never Open Antiques." The shop was part business and part hobby, and she was determined to set limits on public access to her personal time. When customers complained that she was never open, she unapologetically smiled and pointed to her business sign. Although there was a certain amount of humor intended with the name she gave her business, it was also a clear statement of how available she was willing to be.

We're not responsible for keeping doors open for others, but we *are* responsible for not closing the doors to our own good. I wanted to be open enough hours to properly serve my clientele so that in return, they could serve me through an abundance of sales. If a profitable business was my dream, the key to manifesting that dream was making sure I kept the door to my own success open.

Keeping doors open isn't always easy. Even if we don't intentionally close them, they can shut (and even lock) behind us when we're not paying attention. They aren't just the portals to financial prosperity; they're also the ones that lead to personal fulfillment and long-term happiness.

I never met my mother's father—he died when my mother was young—but there was no shortage of stories detailing his varied adventures, and it was through them that I got to know him very well. One story always so intrigued me that I made my grandmother retell it, again and again. It became my personal fairytale.

Once upon a time (around 1919), there was a kindly family man who was an up-and-coming graphic artist for a burgeoning studio in the Midwest. This man (oh, yes, who happened to be my grandfather) had glorious plans for his future, which included both unlimited freedom to express himself as an artist and a healthy bank account. When his company hired a charismatic young apprentice whom he felt shared his drive, he was both delighted and intrigued. Although ten years his senior, my grandfather quickly became friends with this amiable young man. They could often be found after hours, in one of the empty offices, engaged in animated conversation with each other, discussing the details of some wildly creative new project. The new artist had a no-holds-barred vision for his future, and truly believed he could achieve any goal he set for himself.

Because my grandfather felt there was nothing that could keep this confident, talented artist from realizing his "impossible" dreams, he was not concerned when the enthusiastic apprentice was laid off after only a short time with the company.

A few years went by, but my grandfather never forgot the young man with the high hopes, and often wondered how he was getting on. He was both pleased and surprised when he received a letter from the artist, who, by that time, was living and working in California. He was involved in what he described as a daring, ground-breaking, new venture and invited my grandfather to join him in his pursuit of a magical future.

Grandfather politely declined, citing family obligations. The two men shared the same desire for success, and the offer was inviting, but my grandfather wasn't ready to take such a big risk. He had a new family to support, and uprooting them to chase what could end up being an impossible dream two thousand miles from home seemed irresponsible.

The young man didn't give up on his old friend. Twice more he wrote to my grandfather, inviting him to come to California to work with him on his exciting new project. Two more times, Grandfather politely declined. With his "*Closed* sign" clearly displayed, he turned his back on what he knew *could* have been a life-changing new adventure and chose, instead, to play it safe. In doing so, he unwittingly locked himself in his comfort zone and out of the future he so desired. That young artist, Walt Disney, wished upon a star, tucked his *Open* sign under his arm, and went on to make his wildest dreams come true.

Now, interestingly, my grandfather was also named Walt. "The Tale of the Two Walts" has been passed down through the family for several decades—a reminder that anything is possible as long as we keep our *Open* signs out. We alone are responsible for our *Happy Ever After*. Grandfather's story was a huge lesson in what might have been.

As a child, the "might have been" I focused on was the lifetime passes to Disneyland®, which surely would have been part of his retirement package (and which, of course, would be handed down from generation to generation with as much care as the family jewels). As an adult, my expanded perspective allowed me to see the larger lessons, but there are still days when pictures of Cinderella's Castle reduce me to tears.

Clearly, my grandfather was neither ready, nor willing to turn over his *Closed* sign. He wanted his dreams to manifest on his own terms and none of those terms involved risk of failure or loss. Can we blame him, though? What would we have done in that same situation? How can anyone ever know for sure what lies ahead? What if we boldly post our *Open* sign and things don't work out the way we want them to? What if we take the gamble and "lose?" Sure, the *Open* sign worked for Walt Disney, but maybe he was just lucky.

But, what if it's not just about winning or losing, succeeding or failing? What if staying open is more about creating opportunities for greater, richer life experiences? When we keep our *Closed* signs up, we attract more *Closed* signs in return. The more closed we are, the more limited our lives become. Those limitations manifest as increasingly formidable barriers that not only stand between us and our eventual happiness, but block our ability to participate fully in the infinite potential that each new day brings. Likewise, the more open we are, the more *Open* signs we will manifest. Fewer roadblocks will appear along our path and our journey will be more enjoyable (as in exciting, luscious, astounding, fulfilling, FUN, etc.).

A simple shift from closed to open can change everything in our lives, including the depth and quality of our relationships.

A charming older lady from Wyoming used to come into my shop at least once a month. Millie had experienced many challenges in her life, most of them revolving around failed marriages and crash-and-burn relationships. She confided to me that she believed she was destined to always be unlucky in love. We laughed, cried, and flipped through old albums of glossy photos together for more than fifteen years and, after listening to all her tales of misfortune, I was beginning to agree with her assessment.

Then, one day, she showed up at the shop absolutely beaming. She announced that, at age seventy-six, she was getting married again, but this time it was to the *right* man. She'd known her fiancé most of her life—they'd been high school sweethearts—and she was elated that they were finally going to be together.

Even in high school, she'd known he was her prince charming. He was everything she'd ever dreamed of: supportive, loving, caring, spiritual, devoted, and owned a white horse. However, when he asked her for her hand in marriage, she turned him down. She didn't think that, at age seventeen, she was ready to ride off into the sunset with anyone. Her mother reminded her that old maids like her Aunt Gertrude led miserable lives, and she should reconsider, but Millie decided to risk spinster status rather than choose hastily. So, she waited until age twenty-two to marry, and it was to someone else. He didn't ride into her life on a white horse, but he did own a brand new Nash Rambler. That marriage failed several years later, as did two others over the next twenty years. Family issues and personal illness only added to her feelings of hopelessness.

However, during her most challenging times, her princely suitor from years gone by would appear, seemingly out of nowhere. Even though he'd moved away decades earlier, he'd return occasionally to visit with friends and family. Those visits somehow always coincided with turning points in her life. She ran into him at a local restaurant right after a divorce was finalized; she encountered him at the neighborhood gas station after her daughter disappeared; and he just "happened" to show up at a corner market shortly after she was diagnosed with cancer.

He'd gotten married himself many years earlier, but he never forgot her and was always kind and supportive during these chance encounters. Then, after not having seen this man for more than fifteen years, he reappeared shortly after her fourth husband passed away. He told her that he, too, had recently lost his spouse and was now alone.

They reignited their long-time friendship, and soon they were inseparable. Two months later, they became engaged, and six months later they were married. They honeymooned in Disneyland® (ouch!) and she brought me a Mickey Mouse® mug that, to this day, taunts me from the top shelf of my kitchen cabinet. She said to me, "You know, he was always there, right under my nose, but I just wasn't open to seeing him." (I can't resist stories that have both a handsome prince and a happy ending.)

Being open and available for a life of realized dreams begins with our single most important relationship—the one we have with our spiritual source. How many hours each day are you willing to set aside for your personal spiritual growth, for your dialogues with God?

"I do want to work with you, God, but let's clarify my availability. After all, I have a busy life. Now, I *am* open from 9:00 a.m. to 10:00 a.m. on Sundays—I'm in church at that time—so it should be easy to find me. After that, it's a little iffy. I may have an hour or two available later in the afternoon, but it will vary from week to week. Now, weekday mornings are usually good for me, but you need to make it early. I like to leave the house between 6:30 a.m. and 7:00 a.m. so I can get ahead of the rush hour traffic and still have time to swing by Dunkin' Donuts® before heading into the office. I occasionally meditate in the early evening, too, so I may be available from 7:00 p.m. to 7:30 p.m., but it would be a good idea to check with me first. If you find me soaking in the tub during that time, please wait until I've had time to work out the knot in my lower back . . . but after that, I'm good."

The very first place we need to post our *Open* sign is smack-dab in the middle of the road to spiritual enlightenment. Being available for Divine guidance requires us to commit to change, to evolve, and to expand our vision of what is possible. If we're willing to trust in spirit and keep our *Open* sign clearly posted, wonderful things can, indeed, manifest in our lives. The guidance and direction we desire appears—sometimes in the most unpredictable places, and in the most surprising ways. But it *always* shows up.

Leaving our *Open* sign out allows us to access all the gifts the universe has to offer, and at some point, the sign becomes unnecessary because there's no longer any door on which to display it.

Make a plan, take a risk and open the door to infinite possibility. What have you got to lose? Being consciously "open for business" means never having to beat yourself up with, "what if."

Postscript

I did eventually buy a sign to hang in my shop window, but it wasn't anything remarkable. It was one of those familiar blue and white two-sided plastic signs that hang from a chain. A quick flip of the chain changed the message from *Open* to *Closed*.

Beneath the sign, however, I posted an after-hours phone number . . . just in case. Then I got caller ID and voice messaging . . . just in case. It was important, I decided, to not confuse always being available to spirit with always being available to anyone with a cell phone.

Limit One Per Person

It's 5:00 a.m. on a snowy mid-October morning and I am standing in a line that reaches three-fourths of the way around the exterior of Wal-Mart. I have on my racing snow boots with more tread than the tires on my car so that I can make a competitive run for the back of the store once the doors open, and snatch one of the "limit one per person—while supplies last" Wii systems.

I have only a vague notion of what a Wii is, but that hasn't stopped me from lining up with one hundred other people in cold, dripping wet weather with only my no-longer-hot Café Mocha to keep me company.

I haven't played a video game in decades (not since my four-year-old beat me at Pong in straight sets), but I'm determined to have one of these Wii things. Why? Because I've been told there aren't enough to go around and I want to make absolutely sure I get mine.

The only thing I can say in my defense is that I play the lack and limitation game less frequently than I used to, but there are still days when I not only can't justify my actions, I'm at a loss to even explain them.

When I begin to fear that there is only so much "good" (or goods) to go around, my consciousness becomes infected with thoughts of insufficiency, and my entire way of life is dictated by the belief that I must struggle or compete for my share of an ever-dwindling pie. When I mistakenly conclude that the universe is limited in some way, what really does dwindle is my ability to enjoy the lavish abundance that is mine for the asking.

Those *Limit One Per Person* signs were undoubtedly the brainchild of some marketing guru who observed that most people respond better to scarcity than to supply. We may want what we believe we can't have, but once we realize we can have everything, we want for nothing.

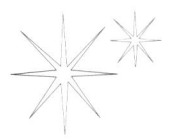
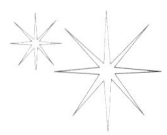

CHAPTER

2

A not-enough consciousness manifests in all sorts of crazy ways, which include everything from obsessive acquiring to all-out hoarding. The mass infatuation with Beanie Baby stuffed animals in the late 1990s was the perfect example of this "must-have/can't-live-without" phenomenon. Elaborate deceptions, unlikely alliances, and creative conspiracies thrived as over-eager Beanie addicts plotted to find ways around the "Limit One Per Person" policy adopted by most retailers. As a small shop owner, it was the best of times and the worst of times: the profit was nice, but the process was a nightmare. The over-the-top demand for these furry toys wreaked havoc in my retail life by shifting my job description from shop owner to head of crowd control (and occasionally heartless bouncer). When the word got out that a shipment of the coveted little animals had arrived at the store—and word always *did* seem to get out—it initiated a stampede of crazed customers. People suddenly appeared out of nowhere, $6.36 clutched in their fearful fists, desperate to acquire another critter for their collections.

At the height of the phenomenon, customers camped out in front of the shop in makeshift shelters, sleeping on bulky back-packs stuffed with overnight survival supplies in order to be first in line when the store opened the next day. At the urging of the mall's management and neighboring businesses, we imple-mented a no-reason-to-get-here-early, luck-of-the-draw lottery system to discourage people from lining up in advance, but it had little effect. On "Beanie Bizarre" days, I would arrive at the shopping center to find anywhere from fifty to one hundred and fifty people backed up on the sidewalk. All eyes would be fixat-ed on me as I exited my car, fumbled with my purse, and made the long, asphalt journey across the parking lot, past the throng of anxious customers to the front door of the shop. A hush would come over the crowd as I inserted my key in the lock, entered the store, and signaled to my staff to take their battle stations. A cry rang out through the crowd as I flipped over the "Open" sign in the window, signaling the official start of the stampede. The rest was always a blur—people, money, stuffed toys, tears, cries for help . . . and that was just my employees. My husband was draft-ed into service as chief of the "beanie police," mediating heated arguments between overly-eager customers while trying to maintain order in the long lines. "Discreet" trades were being made out of the Beanie-packed trunks of cars lined up in the parking lot. The bolder, and often spirited, cash transactions that took place after customers exited the shop with their bagged animal kept mall security hopping. It was retail insanity fueled by the fear that there wasn't enough to go around, that the toy industry was suddenly experiencing a shortage of plush fabric and beanbag pellets.

People created the craze with crazy behavior. Although millions of Beanie Babies were produced and marketed by the manufacturer—enough for every family in America to adopt at least a couple—it was the perception of scarcity that kept them scarce. Once that perception changed and the insanity ended, the floppy pets were everywhere, over-populating store shelves and cluttering up storage rooms.

The fear that there isn't enough—whether it's Beanie Babies®, video games, or the latest incarnation of cell phones—transforms otherwise rational human beings into frightened, insecure Nuts. (As in Nuts the Beanie Baby squirrel . . .)

My mother grew up during the Great Depression. Like many other families, her parents struggled to put food on the table and there was rarely extra money for even the smallest of indulgences. As she grew into adulthood, she carried with her a deep fear that at any moment, everything she had could be snatched from her without warning. As a result, I grew up in a household where absolutely nothing was ever discarded, and having three or four of some "critical" item stashed away in the back of a cabinet "just in case" was viewed as being prepared. Even after she became financially secure later in her life, she continued to jam all the closets in the house with extras of everything from potato peelers to shower caps. Once the closets began to overflow, and there was simply no room for even one more embroidered Christmas-themed guest towel, she would turn her attention to her decorative collections. As long as she kept installing shelves and stacking display cases on top of each other, there was always room for one more fine china teacup, one more smiling porcelain doll, or one more couture-costumed teddy bear with a designer hat. I not only accepted her seemingly benign case of hoarding disease, but I also unwittingly encouraged it, buying her something new every birthday and holiday to add to one of her burgeoning collections. The "not-enoughness" of her childhood grew into a deep-seated fear that the universe wasn't really abundant and the adage claiming that "God will provide" was naively optimistic at best.

I realized I'd been infected with the accumulating disease myself as the drawers in my bedroom dressers began to collapse under the weight of all the can't-do-without stuff I kept jamming into them after my closets became too overburdened to accept any more abundance. All eleven hundred and forty two square feet of my unfinished basement was overrun with boxes stacked within inches of the ceiling, many of which hadn't been opened in close to twenty years. It was disconcerting. My moment of truth, however, came the day I decided to finally clean out my kitchen cabinets.

I was annoyed with myself, but not totally shocked, when I discovered four pizza cutters in my utensil drawer. After all, I was just carrying on a treasured family tradition. I took a deep breath and tossed the three back-up cutters into my donation box and moved on to the shelves in the island. Five redundant glass bud vases later, I was ready to tackle the hanging cabinet with my everyday glassware. The bottom three shelves were simple. They were low enough that I could easily tidy and toss without the aid of a step ladder. In record time, I'd discarded all the extra juice glasses and mismatched wine goblets. The top shelf, however, was out of reach, so I climbed up on a kitchen chair (the ladder was being held captive in the booby-trapped storage closet) and prepared to sort through what appeared to be a random collection of coffee mugs. The frontmost cup was one of those "free refill" mugs that fast food restaurants offer from time to time. My daughter had purchased it for me many years ago as a surprise gift, bursting with pride that the colorfully decorated glass mug she bought for only a dollar would provide me with free coffee for the rest of my life. I had affectionately named it my "'til death do us part" mug and I wasn't kidding. It had been put into service hundreds of times already; I was a fast food restaurant owner's worst nightmare: someone who held on to one of those bottomless refill cups for more than two decades and showed no sign of retiring it to the trash bin. My mother would have been proud, and, in truth, recognizing abundance when it's offered is a key part of establishing a healthy prosperity consciousness, I reminded myself.

Setting the "partner-for-life" mug aside, I dug deeper into the cabinet. I was surprised to find another identical mug hiding behind the first. Hmm, I thought, I must have picked this one up at a garage sale at some point, thinking it would be nice to have a backup in case the first one broke. Being prepared for "emergencies," I reasoned, was a good thing. Planning ahead was prudent, and having one extra of something both fragile and valuable was *not* an indication that I had lost my faith in the abundance of the universe. I almost had myself convinced. Then I found a third mug. It was a slightly different design, probably issued a couple of years after the others, but it was from the same fast food chain and served the same purpose. I struggled a little at first, but ultimately succeeded in justifying how having an alternative design option in my unlimited coffee mug set might be nice. After all, a little variety keeps things interesting.

By the time I uncovered the fourth mug, I was running out of rationalizations. By the fifth, sixth, seventh, eighth, ninth, tenth, eleventh, twelfth, and finally thirteenth mug, I realized it was time for a collection confession. I was a hoarder. One was abundance; a baker's dozen was a backup plan born out of a fear-based consciousness of scarcity and limitation. I was way beyond the "What if one breaks?" stage. I'd moved on to, "What if two break, or three break, or twelve break? Will there ever be another?"

Having thirteen unlimited refill coffee mugs for the same fast food restaurant made me the poster child for poverty consciousness. I was in trouble: clearly it was time for an intervention.

What made the whole thing even more absurd was that, since I now qualified for a senior discount, my free-coffee mug only saved me a couple of quarters. That meant I had thirteen mugs stashed away in my cabinet to ensure that I would never again have to open my purse and surrender a few coins for a hot beverage. Somewhere along the way, I hadn't just lost sight of the big picture. I'd blacked it out completely!

It doesn't matter whether it's what we really want or not. What we give our attention to expands. The plethora of glass mugs in my kitchen cabinet was a testament to exactly how this principle works—literally. Just as one mug led to one more and one more and one more, one doubt born out of a consciousness of "not-enoughness" leads to two doubts and three doubts and four doubts and so on, and before we know it, that bright future we're wanting becomes increasingly doubtful.

Our limiting thoughts are based on the presumption that the supply of what we want—whatever it may be—will eventually be depleted, and we will be left wanting. Is that true? Certainly, some things may seem to be in limited supply in the short run: we may face fuel shortages, electrical blackouts, and occasional empty spaces on the grocery store shelves where they keep, oh, let's say . . . our favorite candy bar with almonds and sweetened coconut dipped in creamy dark chocolate . . . okay, maybe that's just me.

But I have heard complaints from many of my friends (and personally experienced it myself) that it's almost impossible to purchase a ready-made vegetable tray at the local markets the day before Thanksgiving (or Christmas, or New Year's, or Super Bowl Sunday, or any local graduation days, etc.) unless they planned ahead and pre-ordered.

At other times, they're stacked ten deep.

Are we really going to run out of celery and baby carrots in the long run? Probably not. In fact, even during the holiday season, there are plenty of crunchy veggies available in the produce department; they're just not arranged on a convenient round tray with a mega-calorie ranch dip packed in the center. If we're willing to cut our own vegetables and put them on a tray at home, there's no shortage at all. The dip is optional, but there's plenty in Aisle Six if we choose to indulge. It really does become a matter of perception.

A close friend called recently to tell me about her amiable new neighbor, Anne, who had just moved in next door. My friend was apparently very impressed with Anne's "résumé." She'd only spent two hours with this woman, but already knew that Anne had a great job she loved, was financially secure, took annual vacations to Mexico and Maui, and frequented a trendy little downtown boutique on a regular basis. As she gushed (a little *too* much) about her newfound friend, I could hear the resentment building in her voice. As the voice on the phone became more and more strained, I was fairly sure she was clenching her teeth as she spoke and undoubtedly had a chokehold on the handset.

From a perspective of personal poverty, it would be easy to find Anne's seemingly picture-perfect lifestyle infuriating. Why her and not me? Did her apparent good luck in *everything* mean there is less available for the rest of us? Did her prosperity mean one less available job, less money to go around, fewer vacations to book, or a shortage of dresses/sweaters/skirts/cute pairs of shoes to add to our wardrobes?

What my friend missed completely was that prosperity (in the person of Anne) had moved in right next door to her. Seeing Anne as a resource for learning, rather than an object of resentment, could have fast-forwarded her prosperity learning curve. Instead, she put her energy into obsessing over whether Anne had accessed more than her fair share of good things.

I remember reading about a local man who won the state lottery twice in the same year. It made the front page of the newspaper and became the topic of conversation in the lunchroom at work for more than a week. With all the millions of deserving people out there, why did he get to win twice? The "Limit One Per Customer" rule was clearly being referenced.

Sometimes it's difficult to step back and see that we live in an abundant universe. It's *easy* to so focus on the thing (or things) we fear we can't have that we fail to notice all the other possibilities in abundant supply everywhere we're not looking.

I always find it interesting how young children seem to find money on the ground when adults pass it by without noticing. Of course, they *are* closer to the ground than us tall people, and they rarely find anything more than a dollar, but my son, at age seven, always had his secret shoebox filled with cold, hard cash, and it never occurred to him that the universe was anything but bountiful. He never passed on even a penny. When someone told him they were "pennies from Heaven," he smiled and said, "I don't care where they come from as long as they keep falling where I can find them." He loved filling his pocket with the day's "unexpected" prosperity. He didn't worry about whether his friend Andy had more available cash than he did, and he didn't hoard his pennies in fear that people would suddenly stop dropping pocket change. Some days, there seemed to be more abandoned coins available than others, but he never lost faith. He didn't have hundreds of dollars stashed away, but his prosperity consciousness was as big as he needed it to be. His "needs" were limited to one or two packs of football cards a week, and he always had enough to meet his goal.

Somehow, as we grow older, we stop trusting that there is always enough of whatever it is we desire. As long as we're focusing on a potential lack of something in our lives—whether it's coffee, carrots, cash, or anything else—we become blind to the unlimited supply that is everywhere around us. It is fear that begets lack which, in turn, begets more fear. When we feel the need to "limit one per person," we are validating that fear. Fear affirms the possibility of limitation; faith acknowledges the promise of abundance.

We can start building faith from the ground up, literally, like kids do. Look for the "penny" that can create the foundation for the plenty. I don't know anyone who hoards pennies, or who covets the pennies of others. Why? Because we truly believe they are in unlimited supply. There's always a penny lying around somewhere. That principle is not limited to just financial prosperity, either. There are pennies of loving relationships, pennies of radiant good health, pennies of perfect employment, and so on. Abundance can show up anywhere and everywhere.

The first big step in manifesting a little abundance in our lives—and tearing down those *Limit One Per Person* signs—is to begin actually *looking* for those pennies. We can't have what we don't seek out. Once we start looking, those pennies we've passed over, again and again, will begin to attract our attention. Then, finally, we need to complete the process by picking up the pennies we discover. Dismissing them as worthless negates all our hard work.

I love the old saying, "Find a penny, pick it up; all day long you'll have good luck." Luck is simply abundance manifesting—in a small way at first, but in greater and greater supply as those "pennies" turn into quarters, which turn into whatever we have the consciousness to accept. It's a new paradigm that can become the sign of *our* times if we choose to embrace it.

Clean out your cabinets, take your extra clothes, toys, etc., to your favorite charity, and put your energy back where it belongs—on the bigger picture—the one that allows us to see that lavish, unfailing abundance is the true nature of the universe.

Please Obey Posted Signs

Road signs have always been a little confusing to me. Some signs prompt me to move along, while others command that I stay right where I am. They're all pretty insistent and demanding, but I have noticed that there are more signs screaming "no" than those exclaiming "yes," that there are more posted instructions telling me what I *shouldn't* do than those telling me what I *should*. And even when a sign *appears* to be encouraging me to make some forward progress, there are dozens of others that seem to be telling me the exact opposite.

For example, I'm being told to **Proceed**, but **With Caution**, and to be aware of hindrances like Lane **Closed Ahead, No Outlet**, or **Do Not Enter**.

Watch for Oncoming Traffic makes me afraid to even turn on the engine, and once I do commit to becoming part of the stream, even more daunting obstacles can appear without warning, like **Road Narrows, Impassable During High Water,** and **Bridge Out.** If I finally muster up enough courage to just "go for it," I encounter **Obey the Speed Limit.** Which limit would that be? That seems to change constantly—**Speed Limit 20, Speed Limit 75, Speed Limit 35, Speed Limit 50**—up, down, up, down. Speed up, slow down. Slow down seems the safer option, but if I slow down, I have to deal with **Slower Traffic Keep Right.** Right where?

So perhaps it makes more sense to stop and wait for clearer instructions, yet as soon as I do that, I come face to face with **No Parking** and **Tow Away Zone.** And then, of course, there's the big red father of all signs—**STOP!**

Wow, where to go? What to do? Start, stop, do NOT do this, do NOT do that. I want to **Obey Posted Signs,** but it's exhausting. And it isn't just the rules of the road either; there are demanding signs everywhere—all shouting instructions at me.

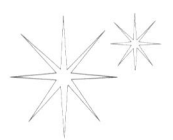
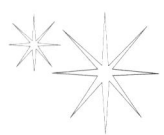

CHAPTER

3

Life has rules and lots of them. Most of our rules, at least the modern ones, are downright confusing. Things were simpler back in Biblical times. Moses emerged from the mountain with ten easy-to-understand "Signs" that were to be "posted" and obeyed. We refer to them as commandments—not negotiable, and not to be ignored.

These rules governed the road of life, not the highway that takes you through the middle of Nevada, but the idea is basically the same.

The Ten Commandments warned us that stealing, cheating, lying, killing, and so forth have some "slap-you-upside-of-the-head" real-life consequences that are hard to ignore. Here in the 21st century, those might include anything from loss of relationships to physical injury to serious jail time, and that doesn't even begin to address all the ways karma can impact our learning curve. So, yes, it's serious stuff.

However, regardless of whether we're talking about "Thou shall not commit adultery" or "Thou shall not go the wrong way on a one-way street," the point is the same—there are consequences for our inappropriate actions, some more tangible than others, but all potentially painful.

My maternal grandmother was a very pragmatic woman. She grew up in Luxembourg in the late 1800s and was raised in a strict Catholic home. She was taught that a life that was neither easy nor "fair" was the natural order of things and the sooner you learned to quit whining the happier you'd be.

Life has rules, she would tell me, rules that must be obeyed, even if you have absolutely no idea what they are. They may or may not be posted somewhere, but it doesn't matter. They are as unbending as the laws of mathematics and ignorance of those laws doesn't change the results, i.e., exempt you from the consequences. And until you learn the rules and put them into practice, you are going to be working with a lot of complex equations and a boatload of negative numbers. This was what she referred to as the "school of hard knocks" method of learning based on the trial and error principle.

With that in mind, she would offer to share her insights gleaned from decades of wrong turns and dead ends, but as a teenager who knew everything, I wasn't interested. What could she possibly know that I couldn't figure out for myself? Well, nothing actually, but that wasn't the point; I could have saved myself a lot of time, heartache, and "hard knocks" by utilizing her wisdom and fast-tracking my life lessons. Instead, like most of us, I chose to learn every one of the rules all by myself, one negative experience at a time.

The "rules" are part of the pesky "It's No One's Fault But Your Own" principle—a corollary of the Law of Cause and Effect. Maybe you didn't know the speed limit on that back road you took to the health club was 45 mph, but doing 60 mph will still get you a traffic ticket if, of course, you get caught, and you always do on some level, but that's a whole other conversation. A ticket is a paper version of an "effect"—a relatively simple one that can be fixed with an apology and a little cash. Not all our consequences are as painless.

Although it's true that sometimes there's a grace period between our actions and the inevitable repercussions, it is just as likely that our consequences will smack us upside of the head, demanding our attention sooner rather than later. Some people are quick studies, while others need multiple reminders before the message gets through.

I have a close friend who is one of those people for whom consequences manifest almost immediately. She breaks a rule of *any* kind—consciously or unconsciously—and she's instantaneously knocked on her butt by the fallout. She gets pulled over by the police on her way to the DMV to renew the license that expired the day before; she is routinely stood up by dates she allows her ex-husband to arrange; and she misses an important job interview because she not only forgot to set her alarm clock, she didn't even remember to plug it in!

She calls it bad karma; I call it a whole lot of things—some of which probably requires professional counseling—but in terms of how the universe works, I'd label it instant feedback. At least she doesn't have to endure years of trial and error before learning where she went wrong.

We all have that friend or family member whose life plays out like a badly written (and acted) soap opera. The consequences of their poor choices and general disregard for the order of things have resulted in a life filled with bruising experiences and weighty drama.

The hardest part of being in that person's life is watching them shoot themselves in *both* feet over and over again, with the same predictable consequences and the same creative excuses. We, of course, would never act so foolishly. "When will they get it?" we lament, shaking our heads in disbelief as we hide the Visa bill under the pillow so our husband won't find it, secretly hoping the credit card fairy will whisk it away to the Land of Debt-Forgiveness during the night.

Simply learning the "rules" is not enough. Until we've mastered incorporating them into our everyday life, it's just a lot of information all dressed up with no place to go.

Taking that next step is essential, but not always easy. For example, I absolutely know that indulging my craving for double chocolate *everything* by whizzing past the salad portion of the buffet in order to be first in line at the dessert table, is going to result in some first class drama at the scale the next morning, but it doesn't seem to dampen my enthusiasm for that Death By Chocolate torte beckoning me from the mirrored turntable at the far corner of the dining room. Yes, I *do* understand the concept of calories, the dangers of fat in my diet, and the monetary cost of letting out my skirts, but I still eat the cake. Then I spend the next week bemoaning the fact that life isn't fair. Actually, it's extremely fair and annoyingly predictable. That's what really upsets us.

Some people call examining our choices and actions a reality check, but who knows what reality really is?—so let's call it a cause-and-effect inventory or a "what were you thinking?" list. If we are willing to examine the effects we're living with, we can usually determine their cause with an open mind and a little detective work.

The ultimate effect of ignoring the laws is that we're miserable: we don't have what we want physically, emotionally, and spiritually. Financial problems, relationship problems, job problems, health problems, and most other problems are a clear indication that we either don't understand the rules or are tap dancing around them.

So, what exactly are those rules? Surely there has to be a better way to figure them out than through one unpleasant, and often disastrous, consequence after another. Combining my grandmother's hard knocks wisdom with lessons learned from a few miscalculations of my own, I think I may be onto something. See what you think.

First of all, the rules aren't as complicated as we all think. Ten laws may have been the norm back in antiquity, but I think they can actually be streamlined down to six with a couple of corollaries. Not paying attention to these tried and true principles won't end us up in Hell (whatever that may look like for you), but it could result in a hell of a time getting the life we desire.

These principles have been around for centuries, but over the years they seem to have lost something in translation. Post these on your refrigerator and see if life doesn't get just a little easier.

Rule #1: **Maintain a healthy spiritual life.**

Translation: **When God speaks, put down the cell phone and listen.**

Life is not all about you, at least not the "you" that is being powered by your ego. There is something greater than yourself that is operating in, around, and through you. It's important to acknowledge and honor that power (let's just call it God), because it knows more than you do and has a better grasp of the greater picture.

Rule #2: **Love Your Fellow Man.**

Translation: **Love people just the way they are . . . even the ones that really annoy you.**

It is not our job to fix people *or* situations. We all have our own paths and need to make our own mistakes. There is a reason there have always been harsh penalties for copying the answers from someone else's test. It's also not appropriate to take that test for them, or try to alter their final score. Basically, we can't cheat our way through life because we'll never actually learn the required material.

It is also not our job to judge other people's choices or decisions. Everyone gets to screw up all by themselves. Every choice has its own consequences; once their consequences become too uncomfortable, they will eventually make other choices . . . or they won't. We can't protect people from themselves.

Corollary: Self-love is the foundation of all true love. When the Beatles sang, "All you need is love," they were insightful beyond their years and may actually have proven themselves to be worth every penny of the staggering amount of money they made. You can only love and accept others to the extent that you can love and accept yourself.

Don't try to fix yourself, because you're not broken. Instead, empower yourself with loving thoughts that honor everything that is Divine within you. Give yourself permission to tap into your own internal wisdom and find your personal path. Then get on it . . . and never look back.

Rule #3: **Give cheerfully**.

Translation: **Be generous with others and quit keeping score**.

We always have something we can give to every person we encounter and every situation we experience. The experience of giving of ourselves in support of others enriches our lives and builds loving relationships.

Giving cheerfully means that we provide support without any expectation of receiving something in return. As soon as we start looking for "payment" on any level, we have to set the unconditional love meter back to "0" and start all over. Expectations of a return on our investment (of time, money, love, etc.) breed resentment, and resentment breeds discord, and discord breeds anger, and . . . well, you can see where this is going.

Giving is its own reward (yes, that adage really is true) but if that gift is also reciprocated, it's an opportunity for celebration and gratitude. And once you understand how this all works, you clear the way for more good than you could possibly imagine.

Rule #4: **Be grateful.**

Translation: **Give thanks for *everything* and *everyone* in your life, including your family . . . *all* of them.**

Life doesn't owe us anything. Clinging to a sense of entitlement does nothing more than give us something to whine about, setting us up for disappointment. Every minute of every day, every experience, every interaction is a gift. Being able to see the hundreds of gifts we receive every single day keeps us in an attitude of gratitude and out of the deep well of self-pity.

Be grateful for the many things that go right every day rather than focusing on the many things that appear to go wrong. How many of those "wrong" things were merely consequences of our ignoring one of the basic rules anyway? Even the "wrong" experiences have something to teach us, and there is an opportunity for gratitude in the gift of learning.

Corollary: Be grateful for your ability to be grateful. Understanding the importance of gratitude in progressing along our personal paths is a huge breakthrough in and of itself. Being able to recognize what we have to be grateful *for* opens the door to a joy-filled life.

Rule #5: **Practice Peace.**

Translation: **Live, let live, and forgive, especially those who don't see things your way.**

Peace is a way of life, not just a cause to be championed. It's not something you rally for on weekends or paid holidays; it's something you choose to incorporate into your life every single day. Allowing ourselves to remain in constant turmoil—angry about this, frustrated about that—not only keeps us up at night, but also compromises our ability to be happy. Remaining peaceful with ourselves and with others involves learning not only to forgive, but also to integrate into our psyches the insights that forgiveness offers us.

Rule #6: **Commit to Spiritual growth.**

Translation: **Stop complaining and do the work.**

We can talk to the point of exhaustion about how the universe works and what we need to do to empower our lives, but if we're only looking for short-term weekend wisdom that can be put back on the shelf come Monday morning, we're setting ourselves up for long-term failure. Taking our own personal inventories on a regular basis—and being honest with ourselves—is one habit you'll never want to break. What's working in my life and what's not? How much of what's not working is simply the consequences of my own thoughts and actions? What do I need to change to get a different result? The trick to mastering the lessons taught by the law of cause and effect is to learn from our consequences early on, so that "a cosmic two-by-four" *doesn't* hit us across the head hard enough to cause blunt force trauma.

I have a personal habit of journaling. I'd like to say I do it *every* day, but that would be an exaggeration to say the least. So, let's say my *goal* is to do it as frequently as possible—twice daily—once in the morning when I first wake up, and then again before I go to bed at night. During both times, I write whatever pops into my head, no matter how dysfunctional or embarrassing it might be.

At the end of the week, I go back and assess that week's "damage." I'm still standing, but what new "truth" could I plug into my life equation to get a more satisfying result?

Every decision we make has consequences, including the choice to write or *read* this book. Hmmm . . . looks like I've become a part of your equation . . . and you of mine. What we do next depends on how ready we are to handle the truth. Thanks, Grandma!

Hazardous Conditions May Exist

I took my first "'til death do us part" vow shortly after I turned twenty-one. Twenty-two years later I exited the marriage. Nobody died—just the relationship. I felt more than a little guilty about reneging on my promise, but I was just barely an adult when I made that commitment, I reminded myself, and didn't fully understand what I was agreeing to. I observed a respectable mourning period and then moved on.

The second time around, I was more cautious about what I promised my life partner. I agreed to "love and to cherish 'til death did us part" . . . as long as all of the following half-dozen conditions were met (failure to do so would immediately render the contract null and void):

1. Never betray my trust, i.e., abuse, infidelity, dishonesty, etc.
2. Never mistreat my children.
3. Never let anyone or anything become more important than our marriage.
4. Never come within 100 feet of me when I'm on the scale weighing myself.
5. Never make me go camping in an old tent . . . with ants and bugs . . . and canned food . . . and wild animals within 10 miles of the campsite.
6. Never **ever** rain on my parade even if I'm the only one marching.

I will love you unconditionally as long as you meet my conditions. Love is never having to ask, "What were you thinking!?"

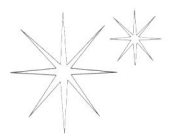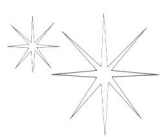

CHAPTER

4

I am proud to say that I'm a true child of the sixties, joyfully spreading love (and flower head-bands) wherever I go. At least, *most* places I go, *most* of the time. I happily share my love with my husband, my children, my grandchildren, my grandpuppies, my extended family, and my closest friends. Occasionally, a new friend that shows promise, or a charismatic stranger with a best-selling spiritual self-help title becomes the recipient of my verbal affection, but it pretty much stops there. I wouldn't want to embarrass myself or anybody else by using the "L" word indiscriminately.

The closest I probably ever came to openly expressing my love to everyone I knew (regardless of race, color, creed, ethnicity, sex, or size of marble collection) was the annual grade school Valentine's Day party. Every year, on February 14th, I would gleefully distribute dozens of heart-themed valentine cards declaring my love for all eighteen to twenty of my classmates, my teacher, the janitor, the school principal, and occasionally, the school secretary, and the lunch lady if I had any extras.

By fourth grade, however, the whole gushy valentine thing was starting to seem a little awkward and card exchanges were limited to best friends only, which absolutely never included any of those creepy creatures known as boys. By seventh grade, the school Valentine's Day ritual was considered too childish for savvy pubescent men and women of the world. The exchanges that did occur were handled in private amid giggles and whispers, and almost always *did* include boys. Love—even the innocent Valentine's Day card-exchange version—became a lot more complicated as I got older.

Somewhere between birth and adolescence, love becomes tainted with fear, fear that the love we give won't be accepted or reciprocated. At age six, I never considered the possibility that someone would refuse my valentine with a curt, "No thanks, I don't really like you that much," or, even worse, pass by my painstakingly decorated cardboard mailbox without dropping in a card. Rejection was still a relatively foreign concept.

Fear never became part of the equation until I realized that other people had the power to hurt me emotionally. I knew about physical pain; my brother Wally routinely whacked me on the head with the butt of his toy pistol every time I changed the TV from *Wagon Train* to *I Love Lucy*.

I also knew about the pain of disappointment and even loss, but I wasn't really exposed to the pain of rejection until I was a little older.

When we're confronted by someone or something that we believe can hurt us, fear of pain sends us hightailing it in the opposite direction. This "threat" can be anything from an angry grizzly bear to an ex-spouse to a particularly insensitive sibling. And not necessarily in that order.

At school, I quickly figured out that the kids who laughed at my over-permed hair, or who told me freckles were the first stages of a terminal skin disease, were not people I wanted to hang around with. Avoidance of emotional pain, even at a young age, is as much common sense as natural instinct. I sought out friends who liked me, regardless of my frizzy locks, my freckle colony, or the oversized black-framed glasses that made me look like a startled hoot owl. Because my equally non-cool friends never made fun of my appearance, I enjoyed being with them. It was the beginning of long and beautiful conditional relationships: ones based on several clear understandings, not the least of which was accepting me the way I was—Toni Home Perms® gone wrong and all.

Conditional relationships are essentially pre-nuptials without the nuptials. They are contracts that are drafted to protect both parties from emotional pain which might manifest in ways such as rejection, loss, disappointment, and insecurity. The more we've been hurt and the more fearful we become, the more contingencies we feel we need to include in our contracts.

When I turned fourteen, my mother sat me down for the obligatory mother-daughter talk about bras, boys, and boundaries. Although the ultimate goal of dating, she explained, was to find someone to marry, it was important to take my time in choosing a life partner and play the field a little. However, I needed to realize that "the field" was loaded with landmines and the ways in which I could get hurt numbered in the hundreds. She then provided me with a list of criteria (all glaringly fear-based) to use in evaluating potential suitors. Her list protected her from what she saw as relationship nightmares in the making. These fears may not have made sense to someone else, but they were extremely logical concerns for her:

Mom's Dating Rule #1: Religious affiliation is critical. I could date any boy I wanted as long as he was Protestant like we were. That meant, of course, that the Italian Catholic boys my cousins hung around with were strictly off-limits, and the Jewish boys in our neighborhood were to never so much as speak my name.

Steering clear of Jewish boys was something of a challenge. Our neighborhood was about ninety-five percent Jewish and our elementary school was a converted kosher pickle factory. On Jewish holidays, my family and the boys from the nearby reform school were the only kids who showed up for classes. It was a narrow field of suitable suitors.

The Fine Print: *Historically, religious wars have always ended badly; even though this conflict would be limited to a relatively (pun* *intentional) few people, she was simply trying to protect me from unnecessary carnage.*

There was also some judgment going on here. "Our" religion had it "right," and other religions, therefore, had it wrong. I wouldn't want to be lured over to the dark side, would I?

Mom's Dating Rule #2: It was important to marry someone who could support me financially. That was because, I assumed, I would never be able to support myself. (I was tempted to call her on that one, but it was hardly worth a rehash of the lecture on men as primary income earners and women, if they chose to work, doing it just for "fun.") "It's just as easy to fall in love with a rich man as with a poor one," she would always say. Although that didn't appear to be true when it came to my dad, her two subsequent husbands had very impressive portfolios.

The Fine Print: *Money buys freedom from insecurity and worry. It also buys the kind of lifestyle that saves you the embarrassment of ever having the "P" word (poor) and your name used in the same sentence.*

She grew up during the Great Depression and knew first-hand what it meant to flirt with the "shame" of poverty. Money also gives you the power to "purchase" protection from the pain of others. Having large amounts of money means you are less likely to suffer the humiliation of being labeled as a "loser," "failure," "reject," and so on.

Mom's Dating Rule #3: Be sure you marry someone who wants to have children. Then have a bunch . . . as soon as possible.

She pointed with pride to the fact that I (her first child) was born nine months and five weeks after she and my father took their vows. "Even if the marriage doesn't work out, at least you'll have children to love you," she counseled. And, if you fall on hard times in your later years, you'll have a *choice* of children you can move in with.

The Fine Print: *The bond between a parent and child is supposed to last forever. Your partner can divorce you, but you will continue to be your kids' Mom/Dad for better or for worse, in sickness and in health, whether they like it or not. Being rejected by a child is an affront to the natural order of things. Having "backup kids" means there's always another child to love you, even if your relationship with one falls apart.*

Mom's Dating Rule #4: Her final condition for a good marriage was possibly the most fear-based of all. Find someone who loves you more than you love him. He'll never leave you *and* he'll bend over backwards to keep you happy.

The Fine Print: *The less attached you are to someone, the less emotional pain they can cause you because . . . well, you simply don't care that much. Likewise, the more attached* they are to you, *the more willing they will be to see things your way in order to avoid the emotional pain you could potentially inflict on* them. *(At least, I think I got that right?)*

Even though I found my mother's set of conditions for a successful marriage (or other long-term relationship) a bit unusual, she was at least very clear about where her fears lay.

By the time I was old enough to start looking for a marriage partner, my list of conditions that husband candidates needed to meet had moved way beyond my mother's four-point agenda. It also included some very specific do's and don'ts—most of which revolved around my own personal fears and insecurities.

My deal-breakers were more about being accepted just the way I was. That included accepting my mood swings even when they gave PMS a bad name, accepting my Type A+ personality, accepting my tendency to fret . . . and fret . . . and fret . . . over my weight, and so on. As time went on, the list grew longer and longer, and I became more and more aware of all the conditions I required to ensure a good match.

We all learn to play the protection game very well. We set up very specific conditions for allowing people into our lives. Then, once we feel sure all loopholes have been closed and all contingencies (at least the ones we can think of) have been considered, we move forward with the relationship. Are we even *capable* of unconditional love? And what kind of love are we talking about here? Are we talking about Love in its purest form (Divine Love, God's Love), or is the word "unconditional" redundant in today's world? Although we may experience brief moments of that level of Love with a capital "L," when we're talking about human love, we're really discussing *loving relationships.* Loving relationships are based on attraction, affection, caring, etc. We *aspire* to Divine Love, and many religions believe that's what we're here to learn, but most of us are still working on mastering human love, on creating loving relationships with fewer and fewer conditions attached. In an unconditional loving relationship, agreements wouldn't even be required. It would be understood that no matter what either party said, thought, or did, love would not only survive but thrive. It would be impossible for either partner to invoke fear in the other, because fear would not exist between them. An unconditional loving relationship means never having to explain yourself.

The closest many of us come to that is in our relationships with young babies. How could you not unconditionally love a sweet, innocent child? Newborn babies haven't been around long enough for us to have developed any baggage together.

My relationship with my grandson Aidan was like that. The first moment I laid eyes on him, newly arrived in the world as he was, my heart filled with such deep love and joy that only the streams of tears running down my cheeks could adequately express the flood of emotions streaming forth. This incredible little being was absolutely perfect in every way. My love for him was equally perfect, laced with the Divine, pure, and unconditional.

One weekend, we had an unexpected opportunity to take a few days off from our business and personal schedules to go visit Aidan. When we arrived, it was clear that he wasn't feeling well and showed every sign that he was beginning to teethe. Later that afternoon, after trying unsuccessfully for more than an hour to settle him down, my daughter exhaustedly handed him over to me. "Work your grandma magic with him, Mom. Nothing I'm doing seems to make him happy." Lifting Aidan to my shoulder, I began singing quietly to him while rubbing his back. My magic didn't last for more than a couple of minutes, and he once again began crying and kicking. I rocked him, fed him, walked him, sang to him, cuddled him, played with him, read to him, and soothed his gums. Absolutely nothing worked. With every new approach I tried, he seemed to become increasingly unhappy. In defeat, I handed him back to my daughter.

I was exhausted and overwhelmed. Maybe I wasn't as good with babies as I'd always thought. I loved him so much. Why couldn't he see that and simply melt into my arms so I could soothe and comfort him? I was hurt . . . and that was only the beginning.

Later that day, after he had quieted down a bit, his grandpa and I took turns reading him his favorite stories. Even though he politely gurgled after I finished each page, I was quick to notice that he seemed to like Grandpa's version of *Pat the Bunny* more than mine, giggling and smiling through all twelve cardboard pages. I was just a teensy weensy bit jealous. Between the soothing challenge and the bunny book incident, I was well on my way to planting the first seeds of conditional love with my tiny grandson. I had discovered, quite by accident, that he had the ability to push my insecurity buttons, to cause me to question my worth, my competence, my lovability, and so on . . . With all those buttons activated, he had the ability to hurt me.

The moment I became fearful of my relationship with Aidan, whether or not I was aware of it, I was putting up a wall between him and me. *I want to love you with all of my heart, without hesitancy, Aidan, but this one tiny little condition may need to be addressed: I can't allow you to make me feel like I'm not enough. As long as we understand that, we're going to be just fine. Oh, and, PS: You can't even* appear *to love your* other *grandparents more than me. You just might want to take note of that.*

Here's this little baby, doing exactly what babies do—being himself, fussing when he's uncomfortable, and living completely in the moment, now suddenly being held responsible for my fear issues. Whenever we are *in* fear, we are *out* of love. The moment we allow fear to enter a loving relationship, it ceases to be unconditional.

When I was in my twenties, I met a lovely woman and her husband who had been married for more than forty years. They lived in a spectacular lakeside home in the most upscale neighborhood in town. A newlywed myself, I was in awe of this long, seemingly flawless marriage and its accompanying lavishly prosperous lifestyle. I soon became friends with the wife, spending many chatty hours sharing coffee, crullers, and conversation as Caroline mentored me in the art of successful relationships.

It seemed like she always had some little insights to share—secrets and strategies for ensuring a long and blissful marriage. One Monday morning, after an argument-ridden weekend with my husband, I decided to just ask her, point blank, how she and

Jim got through the difficult times. She laughed a little and said that, honestly, their marriage had been surprisingly free of any major challenges. She attributed their good luck to one simple thing—something she labeled as "unconditional love." Her unconditional love for her husband was the key to their long, blissfully happy marriage.

To illustrate her point, she matter-of-factly shared with me that Jim had an eye for the ladies and had continued to see other women long after they had gotten married. In fact, she said, he'd had numerous affairs.

I must have stared at her in shock for a good half-minute before I panicked and stuffed a whole pastry into my mouth to make sure I didn't blurt out something inappropriate and/or profane.

She appeared to be totally unaware of my growing uneasiness and the rapidly dwindling stack of baked goods in front of me, continuing with her story as though she was relating a favorite fairy tale. This was where unconditional love came in, she said. She knew about these other relationships and was absolutely fine with them, she insisted. She loved him unconditionally and just wanted him to be happy. And that was what had kept them together for so many years, she concluded. If these affairs were important to him, she was more than willing to quietly look the other way. This arrangement had apparently served them well for many years, and Caroline was not the least bit concerned about the "unconventionality" of the situation.

There haven't been a lot of moments in my life where I was at a loss for words, but this was one of them. Dozens of questions were forming in my mind—most of them beginning with What the!!??—but before something could slip out accidentally, I chased down the crammed-in crullers with an entire cup full of hot tea . . . a few floating leaves included. This had nothing to do with me, I kept telling myself; Jim and Caroline obviously had an agreement that worked well for both of them—so well that they were still together after four decades. And so I said nothing in response and we never talked about it again.

It was a particularly blustery October morning a couple of years later (undoubtedly foreshadowing the events that followed) when I received a surprise phone call from Caroline. She said she had something urgent to tell me, but wanted to discuss it in person. I hung up the phone, grabbed my keys off the hook in the laundry room, and ran straight for my car. Within minutes, I was pulling into her driveway.

After inviting me in, she apologized for the frantic phone call, saying that she really didn't mean for me to rush over. As she prepared tea and put out the usual sweet roll assortment, she made awkward small talk, rambling on about everything from the unseasonably nippy weather to the escalating squirrel population. Then suddenly, without warning, she jumped to the part where her fairytale had gone horribly wrong, blurting out that Jim had asked her for a divorce. Apparently, she explained, he'd fallen in love with one of his extramarital affairs and wanted to dissolve their marriage so he could begin a new life with this other woman. I asked her if she was okay. "Of course," she said, "I love him unconditionally and I want him to be happy."

She related to me their short, but civil, conversation in which she wished him well and invited him to bring a U-Haul over to the house and take whatever he wanted. All she asked for, she said, was the dog, the cat and—she paused for a brief moment during which her entire demeanor changed; with brows furrowed, lips curled, and teeth clenched, she then finished her list—and *every single penny* of their assets: the house, the stocks, the real estate, the CDs, the annuities, the bank accounts. . . . With each item she checked off, her voice grew louder and her tone more intense. The perfect relationship was no longer perfect, and apparently, her love for Jim was not as unconditional as she thought.

Although she may not have had any issues with jealousy, and there were no fidelity conditions attached to their relationship/ marriage contract, when her net worth was threatened, she came out with her guns blaring. When it came to her financial security, there were all sorts of conditions—every one of which she was prepared to defend 'til death did they part.'

When couples take those traditional vows, the promise being made is to love each other unconditionally, regardless of the challenges that arise during the marriage. The skyrocketing divorce rate, however, suggests that fewer and fewer couples are able to keep that promise. Unconditional love is more complicated than it appears, and when relationships deteriorate, it is because of a variety of conditions, spoken or unspoken, that were operating in the supposedly **un**conditional partnership.

For over a year, Caroline and Jim's divorce attorneys wrangled over the distribution of assets. In a teeter-totter game of who's got the money, one week Jim held the advantage, the next week Caroline had the upper hand. After many months of heated debate over the distribution of their financial interests, the couple, exhausted, gave up on the divorce process entirely. Jim broke off his relationship with the other woman, and Caroline welcomed him back by throwing an anniversary party complete with a polka band. The guests were dazed and confused with the strange reconciliation, but a merry time was had by all. As it turned out, Jim's fears around money matched those of his wife's. Neither of them was willing to give up their financial security for love . . . or anything else.

Is it even possible to love unconditionally as long as fear is a part of the equation? Does fear destroy our chances at real, meaningful, loving relationships before they even begin? Working to release fear and open our hearts to greater and greater levels of love is the most empowering thing we can do for ourselves and others.

We have moments of greatness—many of them revolve around our children, or our families—and they are to be cherished. Leaning to love unconditionally is the project of a lifetime. It takes practice and a commitment to growth. There are thousands of opportunities in our lives for us to experience, if only for a few moments, that purest form of Love which is grounded in the Divine.

What does it take to get to that place of unconditional loving relationships? It starts with giving that level of love to ourselves. Over the years, my fears of not being accepted had their roots in my own judgment that I wasn't accept-*able*. Every time I sneaked into my mother's bedroom and borrowed her makeup so I could hide my freckles, I was validating what my childhood tormentors had told me, agreeing with them that my dotted countenance was, indeed, unacceptable.

A few years ago, I was asked to do a Valentine's Day talk for a group of seniors in a neighboring town. I decided to have some fun with the over-sixty audience by creating a top ten list of the greatest—or at least, most famous—"lovers" of all time. The names of Romeo and Juliet, Anthony and Cleopatra, and Scarlett O'Hara and Rhett Butler were all thrown into the hat, as were the famous actors and actresses that created these roles, and others equally legendary. However, when we assessed their ability to love their partner and themselves no matter what, the "greatest lovers of all time" turned out to not be so great after all. When all was said and done, only one greatest lover remained on our list, only one incurable romantic had survived the scrutiny: Kermit the frog.

Yes, they laughed too at the suggestion. But consider this: Kermit opens his heart to *everybody*. Have you seen his ragtag circle of friends? He loves them all regardless of sex, color, species, or fabric content; and, though he admits that "it's not easy being green," he finds a way to celebrate his own beauty and uniqueness. The frog sets a good example.

Conditions are the manifestations of fear and are hazardous to all relationships, including the one we have with ourselves. Fear and love cannot occupy the same space at the same time, and when fear gets there first, it's no contest.

Relationships held together by lists and lists of conditions have no way to grow. Fears quickly come between you and the love you want to both give and receive.

As we work through our own fears and get closer to embracing love, everything in life begins to change. We move closer to that Divine relationship where we can live every day knowing we are unconditionally loved and accepted.

Speed Limit Ahead

I never really paid much attention to speed limit signs until I turned fifty. Up until that time, they were simply redundant white rectangular signs with black numerals on them that appeared on every roadway I traveled. They displayed a recommended speed (again and again) for a particular stretch of road. I didn't always feel a need to **heed** the recommendation, but I admired the tenacity of the highway department.

Once I turned the feared five-0, I suddenly became aware of the number fifty showing up everywhere, including on previously disregarded speed limit signs. I had been pre-programmed by my well-meaning friends to view fifty as the beginning of the end.

They threw me an over-the-top, Over-the-Hill party complete with yards of bleak black crepe paper streamers twisting their way through every room in the house, enough black balloons to block out the sun, and one of those twelve-inch diameter black pin-on buttons with the number "50" in tiny white lights that flashed on and off every time I leaned over to cut another piece of my chocolate mud cake with three-inch-thick black icing.

Two days after my landmark birthday celebration, I had my first disturbing over-the-hill experience. On my way to a favorite coffee shop, I encountered a familiar steep hill—one I'd driven up many times before. But this time, just as I reached the crest of the hill and was about to go **over** it, I came face to face with a newly installed speed limit sign—one that hadn't been there two weeks earlier—that said: *Speed Limit 50*. Stunned, I hit the brake and shakily steered the car to the side of the road where I stopped and sat for a few moments to gather my thoughts. I turned to my husband, bent over in laughter in the passenger seat, and whimpered: "Fifty really **is** over the hill and now I even have the sign to prove it."

My husband thought it was so funny he insisted on taking a photo of me standing next to the sign on the downside of the hill. It was a Kodak moment that I've tried hard to forget. I later shredded the photo, along with my AARP membership card, in a sweeping gesture of denial that also involved some old senior prom pictures and a few refrigerator magnets with which to post them. I wasn't amused by the universe's sense of humor.

I avoided that hill for several months and intentionally sought out *Speed Limit 65* and *Speed Limit 75* routes to get where I needed to go. They gave me hope. There had to be life and success beyond fifty, and even beyond sixty-five or seventy-five, and I wasn't about to take my foot off the gas for at least a couple more decades.

In the meantime, I vowed to look into relocating to Texas where *Speed Limit 80* signs still exist or head straight for Speed Limit Nirvana—Germany and its limitless stretches of the Autobahn.

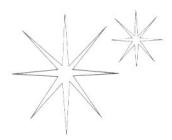
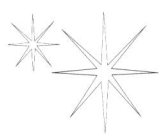

CHAPTER

5

The last place I would have ever expected to spend a Memorial Day weekend was at a NASCAR race. I've never had the slightest interest in car racing; I couldn't name one stock car superstar, and even if I encountered a NASCAR idol in full uniform with his name emblazoned across his jacket, I probably wouldn't recognize him. Yet there I was, on May 26, 2002, at Lowe's Motor Speedway decked out in full NASCAR-fan attire, witnessing a mystifying spectacle known as the Coca-Cola 600.

It was my husband's fault. A few months earlier, during a routine shopping trip to a local discount store, Bob happened upon a small table with an attention-grabbing cardboard display and several pads of entry forms for some kind of contest. He wasn't exactly sure what they were giving away, but there was a familiar red Coca-Cola sign and an enticing counter card that read,

"Win a free vacation." He liked Coke and he loved the idea of a free vacation, so he took a couple of minutes to fill out a form and deposit it in the entry box.

When he got the congratulatory call that he'd won, Bob was excited, but also a little embarrassed. He only vaguely remembered entering the contest and had to ask the effervescent young woman on the other end of the phone exactly *where* we were going for our free trip. After he hung up, he proudly announced that we were heading off to North Carolina to see the Coca-Cola 600, *and* we were getting VIP privileges.

I smiled politely, congratulated my husband on his win, and went back to my office, wondering how I was going to survive four days in hundred-degree heat, hanging out with frenzied race car fans.

I simply couldn't imagine traveling halfway across the country to watch forty drivers race around a track for five hours. I spent way too much of my own time going around in circles. Why would I want to watch someone else do the same? And why would I want to spend an entire day with 167,000 spectators who apparently thought driving around and around the same track four hundred times in a row actually made *sense*?

I did have a very basic understanding of what these races were about: each trip around the track was called a lap, and each one got you closer to the winner's circle, however dizzying the journey might be. What I would come to understand was that this wasn't just some random way to spend a weekend; this was about pushing perceived limits in the pursuit of speed . . . head spinning, heart stopping, unlimited speed.

Just how fast were you allowed to go? On that Memorial Day weekend in Concord, North Carolina, the answer was simple: as fast as technologically possible, and then a little faster still.

The accidental vacation came with the promised VIP treatment. We relaxed at our 3¹/₂-star hotel (with "refreshing pool and massaging spa"), attended festive speed-themed events with feverish fans, and were offered a giddying array of entertainment options, from Jeff Gordon "Cut-Out-Face" photo ops to racecar simulators with deafening sound effects. However, as much as I was enjoying our NASCAR royalty experience, I never planned on going so far as to actually *watch* the race. I tagged along to the stadium, graciously accepted the complimentary souvenir cap with "hook and loop closure for a comfortable fit," a stylish lane-marker-white logo polo shirt, and a "limited edition" collectible die-cast car, and thanked our hosts for their hospitality. Our club seats were cushy and comfortable, crispy cold Coke products and beer were only a few steps away, and enough food to feed a small country was available just down the hallway. I planned to park myself within breeze range of the nearest turbo-charged fan, relax, lose myself in a new book, and take a refreshment break every half-hour or so (whether I needed it or not), while everyone else watched the craziness down on the track.

What I hadn't accounted for was the thunderous roar of the cars as they streaked by, the ear-shattering screams of the high octane crowd, or the wild shaking of the stadium. What I also hadn't expected was just how intoxicatingly exciting it all was. Less than ten minutes into the race, I found myself abandoning my hot-off-the-press reading material and focusing, instead, on the racetrack below. Before I knew it, I was on my feet cheering wildly for Rusty Wallace (he had autographed our hats so it seemed only right to root for him), totally engaged by the spectacle of speed unfolding in front of me.

Standing there with thousands of racing fans, my heart pounding as the cars sped by in a blur of colors and numbers, I began to wonder what it would be like to drive 150 miles an hour (or even more). If just watching the race was this much of an adrenaline rush, how would it feel to actually participate? Going that fast had to be the thrill of a lifetime. I imagined myself behind the wheel of one of those cars—the hot, humid breeze blowing dust through my hair, bugs smashing against my windshield, the smell of burning rubber filling my nostrils. Before I knew it, I was overcome with "speed envy."

Although pursuing a career as a racecar driver would have never made my top ten list of things I want to do in this lifetime, in that moment, I found myself longing for the opportunity to live life largely, full throttle, unfettered by limits of any kind. Would I ever have the courage to create that kind of unbridled experience in my own life, I wondered?

On a recent Saturday morning, I decided to keep track of the number of *Speed Limit* signs I encountered while running errands to the grocery store, the post office, and the overpriced boutique in a nearby shopping center. Although I was out of the house for about three hours, I didn't spend more than a total of thirty minutes actually driving my car. During that relatively short period of time, I came across forty-four speed limit signs (yes, I counted), all demanding my attention. Why hadn't I noticed the sheer volume of these signs before? They had become so much a part of the passing landscape that I was barely aware of their existence. I automatically kept my speed in check without even consciously acknowledging the steady stream of signs flashing their numbers at me. Some of them warned of dire consequences should I exceed their posted limit. Along one stretch of highway, I was confronted three times with a "Fines Doubled for Speeding" notice. I never saw even *one* sign that said, "Fines Doubled for Slow Progress," "Speed Limit Negotiable," or "The Last One to the Mall is a Rotten Egg."

Of course, I realize that those highway-department-approved speed limit signs are put in place with our best interests in mind, and that those limits are necessary to control automobile traffic and prevent accidents.

However, as a metaphor for how we choose to live our lives, they are poignant reminders of how accustomed we've become to living with limitation. We accept the limits we encounter (often self-imposed) without question, slowing down and speeding up, and slowing down again, right on cue.

I know I didn't live my life that way when I was twenty, so what changed? Was it inevitable that, at some point in time, I would stop taking risks, quit using the "passing lane" and leave my "car" in the garage during rush hour? How could I manifest my most treasured desires if I never got my life out of "park?"

Most of us dream large, but live limited. We never dare to slam our accelerators to the floor, risk a windblown bob, and take off for the ride of our lives. Every day, we get into our cars, glance at the speedometer, dismiss even the possibility of experiencing that hundred and twenty miles per hour at the far end of its range, and pull out of our driveways at five miles per hour. We want the ultimate experience, the life overflowing with passion and purpose, but we never get up enough speed to catch up with our dreams.

Do any of these examples of gas-pedal-failure sound familiar? "I've always yearned to be a fine artist, but "artist" is below 200 on the list of best-paying jobs (unless I want to learn how to tattoo something), and I really don't mind working as a computer tech *that* much."
Diagnosis: 120 mph passion with a 40 mph job.

"I'd love to be a teacher, but getting a college degree costs more than my first house, car, and riding lawn mower put together. Besides, it would mean a lot of time away from my wife and kids. So I'll just keep working in my father-in-law's business."
Diagnosis: 120 mph desire with 40 mph vision.

"I'm a great mom and love raising my two children, but I should probably get a *real* job so I can contribute more to the family income."

Diagnosis: 120 mph gift, 40 mph level of self-esteem.

We want all of our fantasies fulfilled, but we're not willing to push our limits, fearful that we may crash and burn on the way to the finish line. That certainly wasn't a concern at Lowe's Motor Speedway.

I had just returned to my seat after grabbing a soft drink from the cooler when, on lap sixty-nine, one of the cars smashed head-on into the wall that separates racers from spectators. Crashes at 150 miles an hour are surreal; tires squealing, sparks flying, metal crunching, and people scattering. Add in the earsplitting roar of the crowd—who immediately rose to their feet to get a better view of the heap of scrap metal formerly known as a racecar—and the moment became both terrifying and riveting. Thankfully, the driver somehow escaped uninjured and was safely escorted off the track. After a few minutes of running under the yellow caution flag (I caught on to the lingo quickly), the cars were back up to speed and the race continued.

Navigating at high speeds has its risks as well as its rewards. Spectacular speeds often equate with even more spectacular crashes. For the remaining drivers on the track that day, the rewards apparently outweighed the risks, because they sped away at the drop of the green flag.

Having the courage to pursue the prize doesn't guarantee a smooth journey. High speeds also increase the wear and tear on the vehicle. Even these multi-million-dollar, high-performance cars break down—engines fail, tires blow out, axles break, etc. Pit crews were called on repeatedly to perform feats of mechanical magic. Even the most seasoned drivers crashed—into walls, fences, and other seasoned drivers. Yet, in spite of heart-stopping moments and what logically should have been race-ending collisions, drivers got right back in their cars and kept on going. No matter how battered and broken his car was, the driver remained in the race as long as he possibly could, intent on crossing the finish line, even if it meant finishing in last place.

My mother would have labeled these NASCAR idols "goal-oriented." I would have countered with "obsessed." Maybe we would both have been right; they knew what they wanted and they pursued it with relentless determination. I thought about the last time *my* car was involved in an accident: a relatively minor collision in a parking lot. I exchanged insurance information with the other driver, drove the limping vehicle the two miles to the repair shop, and called a friend to drive me home. I cursed my forced grounding, begrudgingly rearranged my entire schedule, and put my life on hold until my trusty Malibu was back in service.

At the first sign of a problem, it's easy to pull out of the race and remain on the sidelines . . . sometimes indefinitely. What's *not* easy is working through challenges and getting back on the course. By depending solely on our car to get us to our destination, we forget that the real power lies with the driver. In spite of the fact that these stock cars are technological masterpieces, *they* don't win the races—the people who drive them do.

The drivers don't do it alone, though. Ultimately, the winning car was the one with the best prepared driver and the most effective pit crew. Having a perfectly engineered vehicle was certainly important, but even the best performing cars still needed to stop occasionally for more high-octane fuel and fresh tires. The driver's chances of winning the race were greatly dependent on the skills of his pit crew and their ability to keep him on the track.

Part of our VIP experience was the opportunity to hang out with the pit crew, both before and during the race. Upon arrival, we were immediately escorted to an action-free corner of the pit area where we were less likely to get run over by cars or pit crew workers. During the race, someone was in contact with the driver every second he was on the course, and crew members were poised to act on a moment's notice.

When the driver pulled in for a pit stop, his team sprang into lightning-fast action. As important as the driver's expertise was, he couldn't win the race without a competent, supportive pit crew.

Whether our "pit crew" is our family, our business associates, our faithful Fido, or friends that we refer to as our "peeps," we all have a support system we can tap into. If we feel as though we don't have one, it may be time to start interviewing people (and pets) for the job. When we surround ourselves with others who share our vision, we take an important first step toward achieving our dreams. When we make a commitment to aggressively pursue that dream, we're already halfway to the finish line.

The day before the race, we had an opportunity to tour the garage area. Cars, mechanics, drivers, and wide-eyed onlookers like us were everywhere. It was a small city dedicated to speed. Huge, luxuriously appointed haulers lined the perimeter, and pedestrians were required to yield to cars. As foreign as this all seemed to me, it was clear that this commitment to breaking speed barriers was a lifestyle, not just a weekend job. The success of these drivers was dependent on their ability to completely immerse themselves in the NASCAR culture, where speed consciousness was second nature. We can achieve what we believe is possible. Do you have the consciousness for unlimited speed or are you still creeping along in first gear? When and where do you start posting your own speed limit signs? Are you ready to take them down? How fast are you willing to go?

I returned from my NASCAR experience with a new, no-holds-barred, pedal-to-the-metal approach to living my life. I also returned with a notebook full of race-inspired metaphors I could add to my cache of "the world according to me" new perspectives on the life experience. (They might also work as catchy bumper stickers.)

For example:

"Speed signs may limit my vehicle, but only I limit myself."

"If life is a bowl of cherries, can I spend it in the pits?"

"Cruise control was invented to remind us we can coast through life for a while, but eventually we have to either accelerate or put on the brakes."

"Driving around in circles means never having to think about where you're going."

"To the victor belongs the perfect vehicle."

"Breakthroughs are easier if you're willing to kick a little glass."

"Although there is no I in team, there is also no team unity without U."

"You have to pull up to the starting line before you can even begin to think about taking the checkered flag."

What remains of that NASCAR experience? That hat signed by Rusty Wallace, a few photos of fan favorite Tony Stewart . . . and a commitment to living life without limitation.

Fog Conditions May Exist

Never trust a cat. That, I'm convinced, was Alice's first mistake. To his credit, though, the Cheshire cat was often wiser than he appeared. He advised a befuddled Alice that any road would get her to her destination as long as she didn't know where she was going.

If, like Alice, you find yourself spending most of your time wandering aimlessly in a bizarre universe of your own making, navigating through fields of rabbit holes and hanging out with an odd assortment of mix and match characters, *Fog Conditions May Exist* is your sign. I can relate.

There are two types of fog: real and artificial. Real fog is the kind that rolls in from time to time, but eventually lifts, once again revealing the sun. Artificial, man-made fog, however, is fog juice, a chemical concoction that spews forth from a device called a fog machine. This fog maker can create all the dramatic, scary special effects you desire with the flip of a switch. Of course, I don't really need any high tech electronic devises to create frightening, toxic, foggy environments—my crazy thinking has been doing that for years.

Wandering around in a murky fog of my own creation makes about as much sense as, "Twas brillig and the slithy toves did gyre and gimble in the wabe . . ." When I dump my cache of mental fog juice, the Jabberwocky goes with it, and life starts looking a lot clearer.

Take the blue dress with the starched white pinafore out of your closet, send Alice back to Wonderland, and get clear about who you are and where your spiritual path is leading you. Once you follow directions (don't worry, you're led—always have been, always will be) and pay attention to the signs, all roads lead home.

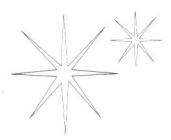 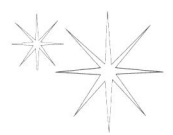

CHAPTER
6

Okay, I admit it . . . I talk to God in my hot tub . . . at night. I share my secrets and vent my frustrations with spirit under cover of darkness. Oh, occasionally, I'll sneak out in the early hours of the morning and stumble, half-awake, half-dressed in some makeshift swimsuit, with a half-full glass of juice clutched in my right hand, stumbling towards the spa-in-a-box. Yes, sometimes I'll go one-on-one with God before the neighbors converge to walk their dogs along the lake, before the joggers hit the dirt path beyond our back yard, when only the mountain ash at the edge of the deck is within earshot of my conversation— *before* I begin another day in the Land of the Lost. But more frequently, it is at night, when there is no chance of surprise interruption or uninvited detection. This is personal, and I want it to remain that way.

My hot tub is considered a four-person spa, assuming we're talking about four very small people with whom you are comfortable being intimate. I know very few people that fall into that category, so I view the tub as best suited for a solo soak. I prefer it that way. Knowing that I may be wandering over to the dark side at some point during the evening's discourse, it feels better not having a lot of witnesses around. Some evenings, I am content to slip quietly into the steaming waters, setting the jets on low and whispering softly to God. On other nights I crank up the jets and the volume, demanding to be acknowledged.

My husband can judge the seriousness of the conversations by the ferocity of the jets. If the waters are bubbling with sufficient power to shake the timbers of our back deck, he knows I'm engaging in a serious Q&A session (aka venting/ranting) with God. He knows to steer clear of me during these periods of intense spiritual dialogue. He lingers behind in the safety of the house, cautiously peering outside from behind the drapes, knowing that anything short of potential drowning would be insufficient cause to get within twenty feet of the raging spa.

These are the times when God and I have it out. I berate the universe for all the things going wrong in my life with questions like, "Why me?", "What does it all mean?", or "What did I ever do to deserve this?" Yelling at God is cathartic. You never know—if I yell loud enough, I might get a real physical sign that someone or something is paying attention.

Once, after a ten-minute tirade on the unfairness of life, the sky above me exploded with a Hollywood-worthy display of flash lightning, complete with sound effects.

I didn't know whether to run inside and alert my husband to the possibility that I'd single-handedly triggered the end-of-days process, or to jump up and down and cheer, "Thank you, God. At least I know you're still listening."

Even on the quieter nights, there are a lot of impassioned whys and whats released into the cosmos; but if I'm tempted to rage on at length, the automatic timer puts an end to the turbulence after thirty minutes, reminding me that staying in my drama serves no positive purpose.

Once the waters calm, I know it's time to make a soggy exit. Getting out of the once hot, but now slightly cooler, water is a feat in itself. Climbing out the side of the spa, grabbing for my moss green, oversized, fluffy towel while straddling the tub's ridge gives new meaning to an ungraceful exit. I know better than to stay in hot water too long, though, and a period of cooling off is ultimately more therapeutic than withering away in the steamy redwood box.

Getting out, drying off, and sealing up the tub again is a ritual of completion. The steam, once rising from the pool, is again captured inside its box, tightly contained by leather straps and plastic latches. The top is just a tad too big. Even after securing it as best I can, an eerie, foggy mist seeps out from under the cover, taunting me as I try to discreetly slip back into the house unnoticed.

I depend on this nightly ritual where I can clear my head of crazy thinking and otherwise errant thoughts. What do I really hope to accomplish each night in the watery confessional? I figure that if I can get clear with spirit on a regular basis, I just may be able to approach the next new day from a slightly more enlightened perspective. "Okay, God, this is what worked; this is what didn't." So I think to myself that tomorrow I'll give it another shot—hopefully with a little more insight.

It's not even so much about getting answers to the lengthy list of questions posed nightly; it's about being willing to at least recognize what those questions are—particularly the ones that continue to surface night after night. I'm aware that the questions posed, the frustrations vented, reflect a continuing internal dialogue that's endeavoring to make sense of who I am and why I'm here. Discerning how I should go about finding my purpose and direction is not always clear. It's often like navigating in a thick, murky fog—and fog can certainly slow down progress.

I don't often venture out into the fog if I can avoid it. Oh, sure, there's a certain mysterious, theatrical appeal—the soupy, thick air that blurs my vision while simultaneously heightening my other senses. Noises are louder in fog, but voices seem softer. Light fails to illuminate more than just what is a couple feet in front of me, and everything is shrouded in mystery. It's oddly exciting at times, but more often evokes a feeling of being hopelessly confused and disoriented.

The dense fog that moves in from time to time is a part of the process of growing and becoming all that I can be, and I've learned to accept and even embrace it when necessary. After all, there is some kind of crazy safety in fog. While it restricts my view, it also protects me; I don't have to deal with that issue two feet in front of me if I don't know it's there, or if I *pretend* I don't know, because my vision is temporarily obscured. Fog can act as a blanket—comfortable, familiar, giving us a place to hide. It allows us to delay committing to any one path; all directions are equally appealing (or daunting) since you can't see what's ahead. As the Cheshire cat quipped, pretty much *any* road will do as long as we have no clue where we're going. There is some odd sort of security in that.

And when there isn't enough natural fog in our lives to provide that security, we find ways to manufacture our own unnatural version.

"Real" man-made fog has been a popular stage convention for centuries. Plays like *Macbeth* would be nothing without fog-dripping settings. With the help of fog machines, the dark smoky stuff can be created and recreated right on cue. Of course, we've been able to create this dark smoky fog with nothing more than our errant thinking for thousands of years. Foggy thinking, empowered by fear, sets in motion a toxic fog-making process that completely obscures our view of everything outside our comfort zone, including the truth of who we are and why we're here.

I met my husband in man-made fog of the stage variety. He was performing in the civic ballet's annual production of *The Nutcracker*, and I was assisting backstage.

I didn't meet Bob personally at that time. I knew him only as the tall butler with heavy makeup and a deep voice. As the manufactured fog filled the already darkened stage, I handed him a cache of magical props, which he greedily accepted and then quickly disappeared once again into the mist. It was one of those strange, chance meetings that neither of us even remembered until we began dating a few years later. Meeting in the dark on a fog-saturated theatrical stage was not only a good "how we met" story with tons of entertainment value for our friends, but it was also an intriguing metaphor for that first encounter. The fog turned out to be an even more appropriate metaphor for where each of us were in our lives at that time. It's a wonder our paths ever crossed again.

If we hadn't chosen to shut down our fog machines and exit our personal dramas, we might still be wandering around in a perpetual haze. Gratefully, we were afforded a chance to reconnect in a fog-free environment. Those opportunities are rare. Often, as the artificial fog dissipates, its natural cousin rolls back in, making it difficult to distinguish between the two.

Being caught in the fog cycle, flipping back and forth between natural and man-made mist, may very well be the perfect example of what it means to be spiritually lost. I know. I've been lost a lot. No sooner do I settle on what I believe are well-thought-through answers to: Who am I? What is my life purpose? What do I need to include in my spiritual practice? Can I really change my life by changing my thinking? Are yoga classes a prerequisite for enlightenment?, then confusion rushes in, and I'm once again wandering aimlessly.

Case in point: even though at age twenty-one my clear vocational choice involved working in professional theatre, I begrudgingly agreed to take a stab at teaching high school. As a senior in college with a major in something as "impractical" as speech and theatre arts, my future didn't look promising—at least that was what my mother and counselors decided. They strongly advised that I consider a backup plan, just in case that career on the New York stage never panned out.

For them, the clear "Plan B" was high school teaching certification. I protested as loudly as I could, pointing out that I'd end up spending most of my time teaching basic English classes with only the annual school play to look forward to. Even if I did get to teach an occasional speech or drama course, working with young teens was outside my comfort zone. I'd barely survived my own teenage angst; why would I willingly put myself in a position where I would be called upon to manage someone else's? They insisted, however, and I gave in.

In September of my senior year, I found myself at a small, rural high school in downstate Illinois standing in front of a room filled with twenty-two sophomores, most of whom didn't really want to be there. That was okay, because I didn't either.

My first class as a student teacher was a solo flight. The supervising teacher introduced me to the group and then made a quick exit out the back door, never to be seen again.

I managed to get through the first five minutes without losing more than fifty percent of the group's attention to note passing and studying the pattern of the ceiling tiles. Teaching grammar was simply not my forte, but I was determined to survive the student teaching experience so I could activate my employment insurance policy. I had barely finished writing my name on the blackboard, when a hand shot up from the back row. Before I could even acknowledge him, the young man blurted out something about it being too hot and stuffy in the room for him to think, and could he please open a couple of windows. It seemed like a benign enough request, and I nodded my approval.

Centering myself at the front of the room, I took a deep breath, and directed the class to focus their attention on me as I prepared to deliver the most inspired explanation of adverbs they'd ever heard. Finally corralling the attention of at least seventy percent of the fifteen-year-olds, I beamed with confidence, glowing with the satisfaction of having control of my classroom. My reign as master teacher lasted exactly thirty-two seconds. The wide-open windows had attracted the attention of a curious pigeon, who chose that exact moment to make a noisy entrance, circle the room, crash into the supply cabinet, take out a plant on an upper shelf, and land, finally—where else—on my head. Then just when I thought things couldn't get any worse, they did.

Without even a hint of remorse, that pesky pigeon did his bird dropping thing . . . on my hair . . . right there in front of twenty-two teenagers, now convulsed in uncontrollable laughter. I finally had a hundred percent of their attention. There was no way to survive that experience with any amount of dignity, and I didn't even try. I managed to somehow complete my student teaching and acquire the coveted certification. Then I left town and changed my name. It was the right thing to do. Oh, and that teaching certificate? I never used it. *When the bird of someone else's happiness poops on your head, you know you've wandered woefully off course, and it's time to seriously re-evaluate your direction.*

Caught up in some foggy reasoning, it was easy to convince myself that I could somehow manifest my own dreams by surrendering to someone else's agenda.

It's that kind of hazy thinking that gets me into hot (tub) water on a nightly basis—literally and quite intentionally. Still, each time I get to voice my concerns, analyze my behavior out loud, and then climb back out on my own power, it feels like I'm just a little closer to finding my way.

It's interesting how the same questions continue to arise, the same frustrations bubble to the surface night after night. I've been caught with the equivalent of that preposterous pigeon on my head numerous times, and I've needed to deal with some messy consequences before I could move on.

All the "why" questions really come down to a plea for clarity, for a clearing out of the mind-fog so I can choose again, more wisely this time. Clarity reveals the truth of who we are, of our highest and best life, our passion, and our joy.

That doesn't mean it's easy to silence the foghorn in the distance. However, once we become aware that *Fog Conditions May Exist* in our lives, it helps if we can distinguish between nature's fog and that of our own making.

Most naturally occurring fog doesn't last long; it burns off as the temperature rises and the sun appears from behind the clouds. Visibility may be temporarily limited, but watching it lift, revealing a clear view of where we're going, can be almost magical.

Artificial fog, on the other hand, with its caustic chemicals and smoky smell, is fear in its most pervasive form, infecting every part of our lives. Artificial fog is little more than premeditated delusion—a foggy way of being in the world that can be maintained for as long as our fog juice supply will allow. Of course, that supply can be continuously replenished. It's a way to avoid making any real decisions, not looking at what the next step might be, and not glancing farther down the road to a possible destination. The machine continues to spill its contents on cue, and while we're basking in the smoky substance, it's easy to blame others—those outside the fog—for being the source of our suffering. We can't look them in the eyes and see our truth reflected back to us when there's too much smoke to reveal the mirror.

The desperate cries of "Why?" and "How?" won't find any resolution until our vision clears. If the fog in your life has simply settled in for a brief visit on a cool fall morning, sit back and wait until it passes, knowing its ability to obscure your vision is fleeting. The sun will eventually shine again, and the world around you will reveal itself, perhaps looking even brighter by contrast. If the cloudy haze has been self-created, though, nothing short of dumping the cache of fog juice and pulling the plug on the machine will be effective. That's a conscious choice, and it's ours to make. Any really meaningful conversations with God are dependent on a willingness to do just that.

Detour

If I ever write my memoirs, I think I'll call them, "Postcards from the Scenic Route."

The "scenic route" was the euphemism my mother used for detours—those inconvenient, frustrating, annoying, long and winding roads you end up taking when the easy, direct route to your destination is closed off. Whether it's a *Bridge Out*, a *Dead End*, or just a big orange *Detour* sign on what appears to be a perfectly good road (apparently placed there just to make life more difficult), it's exasperating.

I'm a magnet for detours. If there's one somewhere within twenty miles of where I'm currently located, it will send out a tractor beam and pull me in its direction, just to be sure I don't miss the opportunity to, once again, take the long way around something.

After decades of zigzagging my way through life to avoid obstacles, I'm not sure I'd know what to do with a direct route if one opened up for me. What? You mean I can actually get there from here? No mountains to climb? No hurdles to leap over? No streams to ford? No trials to survive? No quests to complete? No demons to slay? No True/False test with a bonus essay question to pass?

Detours stop showing up in our lives once **we** quit posting them. The only indirect route to enlightenment is the one that has to navigate past our fears.

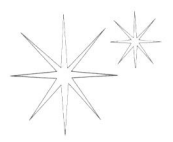
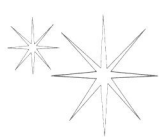

CHAPTER
7

A few years ago, I received a book as a Christmas gift from my daughter, Nicole. I knew it was a book before I even opened the package; it didn't take much detective work. It had the label from a popular book store affixed to the neat gold wrapping just beneath the flat metallic bow. I hadn't *asked* for a book—I was already at least two years behind on my reading, which I was now strictly limiting to spiritual self-help volumes—so I set the gift aside and began opening more promising packages. Nicole was twelve hundred miles away and would never know I left her gift for another day. I eagerly unwrapped the remaining gifts, gushing my gratitude with the dozen or so family members gathered around our new eight-foot, fiberoptic Christmas tree, oohing and aahing as the lights magically morphed from one color to another.

When I finally opened Nicole's small package the next day, I was a little startled and a lot puzzled. I didn't recognize either the title or the author, and it held absolutely no appeal. Too tired to investigate further, I tucked it away on my bookshelf between a well worn copy of *The Tao of Pooh* and my hardbound version of *The Grass is Always Greener Over the Septic Tank* and vowed to remember to send her a polite thank you note for her thoughtfulness. What I didn't do, however, was even crack the cover.

A week later, my daughter called me from Seattle and asked whether I'd read the book yet. I was tempted to lie as lovingly as I could in order to spare her feelings, but I know she has a particularly sensitive crap detector—even over the phone—so I confessed that I hadn't. I could hear her deep sigh on the other end of the line, and, finally, after a few seconds of silence, she asked with as much patience as she could muster, "Mom, did you even get past the title?"

"No," I admitted, feeling a little ashamed. In fact, it was the title that had stopped me short, tying a knot in my stomach that sent me to bed that night clutching a bottle of Pepto Bismol®. It was *because* of the title that the disturbing paperback, with its tauntingly crisp corners, had been immediately relegated to the dustiest bookshelf in the house, where I planned to keep it indefinitely.

It took only a quick glance at the book's cover, which featured an odd looking pair of men's boxer shorts, to know it had nothing to do with self-help, spiritual or otherwise, but that wasn't really what was stopping me. What gave me pause was the large imposing one word title: *Naked*.

Odd as the book choice might seem, Nicole explained, it was the absolutely perfect gift for me, and if I read it I would understand why. She hinted at it having something to do with the potentially terminal bout of writer's block I'd been experiencing for almost a year, but she refused to elaborate. Instead, she strongly encouraged me to give *Naked* a chance, saying that David Sedaris' book was laugh-out-loud funny and brutally honest— an unflinching exercise in self-examination and full exposure.

That's exactly what I expected it to be and precisely why I didn't want to even turn the first page; I knew it was a cleverly disguised Pandora's Box. I wanted nothing to do with getting naked, on any level, in any way, and even my well-meaning daughter wasn't going to get me to change my mind.

I had *never* been particularly comfortable with exposing myself, whether it involved full monty physical nudity or emotional openness—it was all the same, awkward feeling. That fear of "letting it all hang out," was particularly paralyzing when it came to my writing. I wanted to reserve the right to fictionalize my nonfiction as required, to protect the innocent and divert attention away from the guilty. Even the *idea* of getting naked with readers scared me to death. The more people knew about me, the more vulnerable I became to all kinds of judgment, including blistering criticism and humiliating ridicule. I was very secure in my insecurity.

I think it was sometime during puberty that my inadequacy gene fully kicked in, ushering in a painful period of preteen distress replete with self-doubt and personal drama. Although I learned to use my over-the-top, outgoing, energetic personality to mask my growing self-consciousness, I longed for private time alone with my inadequacies, where I could brood in silence to my heart's content.

Privacy, however, was not an option in a crowded apartment overflowing with close-knit family. Little eyes tracked my every move, and the seemingly incessant questions from my adorable, but pesky, younger siblings interrupted any time I tried to set aside to contemplate the meaning of life, or even which plaid pleated skirt I was going to wear to school the next day. I fantasized about long bubble baths and personal spa time, but with only one bathroom for seven people, bathing was, of necessity, a community event—all the girls in the tub, then the boys. Even on those rare occasions when I could bargain with my parents—two hours of babysitting for thirty minutes of solo tub time—I was invariably interrupted by someone outside the door with a pressing need to use the facilities . . . NOW!

And then there was the infamous tub-time-terrorist incident, when my nine-year-old brother hid in the bathroom hamper, patiently waiting for more than a half hour until the perfect moment—just as I stepped into the tub—to pop up and scream demonically, "I see you naked!"

In the bedroom I shared with my two sisters, I couldn't so much as change blouses without younger siblings of both sexes bursting through the door with a motley following of curious neighborhood friends.

My lack of privacy wasn't limited to interrupted wardrobe changes. I could never journal in my diary without a dozen distractions, or the fear that one of my brothers would snatch my "book of secrets" off my lap and parade it up and down the block, putting it up for sale to the highest bidder or the friend with the biggest jar of fresh worms.

Even studying for school became a challenge. Often, my only chance at solitude, fleeting though it was, was to slip behind the front room furniture when no one was looking. There, in the narrow space between the back of the floral upholstered couch and the wall, I read through my social studies assignment as quickly as I could before my brothers showed up for their daily reenactment of Custer's Last Stand, followed by the Gunfight at the O.K. Corral.

While my parents, brothers, and sisters seemed to revel in the Cheaper by the Dozen, large family life-style, I would have preferred to face a firing squad. I favored huddling alone in a corner reading books over happy-family outings in the crowded station wagon where I was exiled to the backward-facing seat that offered a dizzying view of everywhere we'd *been*. I was still in the early stages of obsessive agonizing over my future, but

I was already fairly sure my life purpose did not involve large numbers of children and/or a small bank account. Surely, I was destined for something greater.

I don't know whether it was after I went on the thirty-two-book Napoleonic era reading spree the summer I turned thirteen or the fourth time through my treasured copy of *Gone With the Wind*, but somewhere along the way, I decided that the best way to explore who I was and what I wanted was to learn as much as I could about the lives of others who had achieved "greatness." I wasn't sure if I was more intrigued by the emperor who aspired to rule the world, or the tragic heroine who aspired to rule the men in it, but they both led deliciously exciting lives, far more interesting than mine. So I made the decision to set mine aside. Thus began the "acting" phase of my learning curve.

In high school, I developed a passion for the theatre which followed me to college, where I ended up graduating with a degree in speech and theatre arts. I became very skilled at taking on one persona after another, transforming myself from tragic Greek heroine to crazed American divorcée—and everything in between—at the drop of a curtain.

I continued on to graduate school, where I hoped to add several more identities to my repertoire. So when the head of the theatre department announced tryouts for a production of Shakespeare's *Troilus and Cressida*, I was the first in line at the auditions.

My determination paid off. I won the lead role of Cressida and threw myself into rehearsals with passion and purpose. And then something happened I simply hadn't anticipated. A week into rehearsals, the director called me into his office to share his inspired *new* vision for the production, which he felt would freshen up this dusty old classic. It was "daring" and innovative, he teased, a bold approach that would "wake up" our sleepy, conservative university town. After all, it was the progressive 1970s, he proclaimed, and it was his obligation to explore, through performance art, the current generation's demand for openness and honesty.

I know I must have rolled my eyes at least a couple times during his thirty-five minute oration, but I tried my best to appear genuinely interested and enthusiastic. When he cited productions such as *Hair* and *Oh, Calcutta* as examples of cutting-edge theatre, I should have realized where this was leading, but I didn't. His proposal caught me entirely off guard and very nearly off my chair.

I'm not sure what his exact words were, but essentially what I *heard* was: "I've decided to blow everyone's mind by doing a grab-and-grope, sexually explicit version of the love scene between Troilus and Cressida . . . in the NUDE."

My mouth tried to form words, but I went inexplicably mute. I immediately started twisting my hair (a nervous habit that always kicked in when I was acutely uncomfortable), stared down at the scuffed tile floor for what seemed like an eternity while I prepared an appropriately indignant response, and then, gathering my courage, looked him straight in the eye, and blurted, "Artistic expression, my ass. And by the way, I'm not exposing mine. I didn't sign up to do Shakespeare—or anyone else for that matter—in the nude." He laughed a little, questioned my commitment to my art, and tried to convince me that doing a nude love scene would be a wild and sassy move that could get me noticed by talent scouts. By talent scouts? In Fort Collins, Colorado, with a population of 25,000? In a college play produced by a Theatre Department with a total of three faculty members? Oh, I would get noticed, I insisted, but not by agents looking for Broadway's next big star.

At that time, I was a teaching assistant in the Speech and Theatre Department, where I had two freshman-level public speaking classes. I less-than-calmly explained to him that he was out of his mind if he expected me to get up in front of my speech classes on the Monday morning after opening weekend, knowing that all (or most) of my sixty students had just seen me naked two nights before. I ranted on about just how shocked I was that he was even considering adding gratuitous sex to a revered Shakespearean tragedy, and how outraged I felt at his cock-eyed interpretation of the Bard . . . and then, setting up the big moment . . . I tossed my script on his desk and loudly declared, "I quit; find yourself another naked coed to do your X-rated dirty work!" In hindsight, I may have laid it on too thick, but I needed to set up my dramatic exit from his office, during which I kicked the frail old wood door shut and stormed off down the hall.

There was *no* way I was going to get naked—not for my art, not for some political agenda, and not for this director. There was just so much of me I was willing to share with *anybody*, including, I came to realize, myself . . . and God.

So, here I was, some thirty years later, revisiting these same feelings of extreme embarrassment and discomfort. Only this time, it involved the book I was writing—the one with all the highly personal anecdotes; the one that was demanding that I get naked in front of yet another audience—a readership terrifyingly larger than the hundred or so theatre-goers who would have showed up to those college performances.

The more I wrote, the more naked I began to feel as the layers of protective "garb" were falling away, and the real me was being revealed—all the good, the bad, and the difficult to even acknowledge. Why was I sacrificing my privacy just to complete a book project that was causing me so much discomfort?

Not only was I uncomfortable, I was completely shaken. I shut down creatively and couldn't write for months at a time. I was having difficulty finishing the dozen or so chapters I'd already written, even though I had completed first drafts of every one of them.

Of course, I didn't tell anybody about the source of my writer's block. I crafted, instead, a good story for why the book wasn't getting done. Actually, I had *several* good stories for why the book wasn't getting done—none of which bore any resemblance to the truth, but all of which sounded fairly plausible.

People could take their pick: I was drowning in editing projects; my online business needed me 24-7 just to stay afloat; grading homework for the classes I was teaching kept me up well past first-run television shows (which, of course, I had no time to watch anyway).

When people asked me how my book was coming along, I would joke and say, "You know, a funny thing happened on the way to finishing that book and it was: (fill in the blank)." It worked. Friends would nod their heads in sympathetic understanding, and for two years I was more or less officially released from any obligation to complete my project.

Then a funny thing really *did* happen. As I was packing up after one of my classes, I was confronted by a close friend who suspected I wasn't being entirely forthcoming about my book. "So, how is your book *really* coming along?" he insisted. I felt that familiar hormonal flash of intense heat overcome my entire body, and in the midst of some serious sweating, I began to over-explain (always a sure sign that I was dodging the truth) why the book wasn't done yet. He wasn't buying any of my pat excuses and repeated his question. This time I blurted out that that I'd run headlong into a wall and couldn't find a way to tear it down.

He paused for a moment and then suggested what he thought was the perfect Sign to guide me through my challenge. Maybe, in working through this sign, he counseled, you'll find the insight you need to remove the wall that was growing in size, brick by brick, as each week passed.

I wanted to make a quick exit, or, at the very least, change the subject, but he would have none of it. As uncomfortable as it was, I had to admit that the sign he proposed was right on target. In that awkward moment, it became absolutely clear to me what was standing in the way of not only completing my book, but finally coming to terms with my fears around getting naked.

It was time to complete what I'd put off back in graduate school some thirty years earlier. What I dismissed as setting appropriate boundaries had, over the years, turned into a pattern of constructing impenetrable barricades. What I had insisted was a quest for privacy was simply a smokescreen to divert attention away from my need to shut down and withdraw, to retreat into a dark, moody, private universe of my own misguided creation.

Behind those boundaries-turned-barricades was truth in all its glory (and *ingloriousness*). It was now clear that the time for well dressed, partially clad, or even cleverly disguised truths had long since passed; the time had come for the whole truth and nothing but—or, in other words, buck-naked, full-frontal-nudity-style truth. It didn't feel very good.

The telltale sign that was now demanding my attention was directly in front of me, placed strategically in the very middle of my path. It was impossible to miss. How had I not seen it before?

No, it wasn't *Nude Beach*. No, it wasn't *Dress Code Strictly Enforced*. It wasn't even *Open for Inspection*. It was, instead, *Detour*. It's message? Until I was willing to get "naked" with myself and God, until I was willing to shed the layers of fear—in all its various manifestations—that had been building up for decades, I was going to encounter one detour after another along on the road to enlightenment. That included the "scenic route" I was currently taking on the way to completing my book.

Detours aren't inherently bad. Signs like *Detour* warn of danger ahead allow us to steer clear of potential hazards. We wouldn't want to get stuck in that two-foot-deep pothole, would we? Or attempt to ford that stream where the bridge has been washed out? Or bottom out our vehicle by trying to navigate along a half-completed roadway still under construction? That *Detour* sign keeps us safe in those situations when we simply can't get from where we are to where we want to go without potentially disastrous consequences.

Signs that alter our direction teach us to be patient with ourselves. They also route us around sections of the road that are in the process of repair, and give us time to grow and evolve before moving forward.

The stream of *Detour* signs I was encountering were put there to protect me from my own self-doubt and lack of faith. Before all my insecurities around my ability to write a competent and worthwhile book could manifest in a crushing failure, the *Detour* sign steered me in another direction. I still had a lot to learn before I could move forward successfully. The potholes in the road ahead were the size of the Grand Canyon, and the majority of them were put there by my continued affirmations around who I *wasn't* and what I *couldn't* do. Spirit afforded me as many opportunities as I needed to prove myself right—hence the ever-growing size of the potholes ahead and the increasing length and complexity of the detours.

Every time my writing stalled, every time my inspiration "failed" me, I was able to build a stronger and stronger case against myself. That self-doubt evolved into a pattern of shutting down options and retreating into a place of self-pity before the next leg of my journey had even begun. With time, I became so accustomed to my misery, so resigned to my fate, that the detours leading me away from my goal became a way of being— a very comfortable way of living my life by default.

The danger is that we can become so used to detours that we no longer notice we've been led off course . . . again and again, putting more and more distance between ourselves and our dreams.

What do we need to do to get back on track? What will it take to make an empowering course correction? How many layers of my self-imposed misery do I need to strip away before I can uncover the Truth about who I am, the divine perfection that lies beneath all the appearance of lack and inadequacy, mistakes and failure?

Getting naked with ourselves and our spiritual source is being willing to let go of the familiar (and often oddly satisfying) way of being that keeps our true nature locked away behind the walls of depression, victimization, and hopelessness.

Being willing to strip away pretense and examine who we've become, one layer at a time, is not an invasion of our privacy, but an opportunity to reveal our magnificence.

It has taken me a long time to become comfortable with getting naked, and on certain levels, it's still a challenge. Some types of nudity are definitely reserved for the young and the fit (and that ship not only sailed, but got lost at sea several decades ago). However, I'm making progress with the others.

It is somewhat ironic (heck, maybe even downright funny) that over the years, I have been cast four times in the role of Eve in Mark Twain's *The Diaries of Adam and Eve*. I like to think of this bit of synchronicity as proof positive that God has a sense of humor. I am grateful that I've learned how to laugh.

Taking a long, hard look at who we are, where we've been, and where we want to go as we co-create with God, is a private experience with a very public result, an empowering one that positively impacts everything we do and everyone with whom we interact. As a bonus, it also clears away all those annoying detour signs with their arrows pointed in every direction except up, and reserves the scenic route for flash-happy tourists.

How much we choose to share of that experience is up to us. What we cannot *help* but share is the new way we show up in the world—as open, loving, and at-peace-full beings.

Yield

My name is Linda and I am a control freak. I admit it. There are two kinds of control freaks—those who are in recovery and those who are in denial. I'm both. Before I founded my own personal chapter of CFs Anonymous and voted myself in as president, I trusted no one's judgment but my own and tried to manipulate outcomes.

My relationship with spirit was more one of coercion than a yielding of conscious connection to God/Creator/Source. God, do this for me; God, do that for me; God, make this problem go away. Expecting me to "let go and let God" was like asking a chocoholic to put down her fork and walk away from a double chocolate brownie with triple fudge icing.

I equated power with struggle and I was absolutely convinced that the universe could accomplish nothing without my continuous input. I knew this to be true because things were spiraling downward faster than I could make new lists of demands. So I struggled harder in an attempt to regain control.

Then one day I ran down a *Yield* sign at 80 mph and had an epiphany. "Power struggle" is a contradiction in terms because achieving and maintaining power has nothing to do with struggle.

We don't need to demand power because we already have it; in fact, we have always had it. In yielding to that which is greater than we are, we are able to claim true power—the kind that gives us the ability to not only have everything we desire, but to begin to desire only that which truly empowers and serves our highest good.

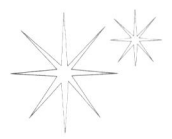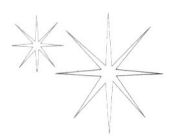

CHAPTER
8

Admittedly, it's been a very long time since anyone has asked me that burning question, "What's your sign?" (1983 perhaps?), but the next time someone does, I plan to trash my clichéd "Taurus" response and get real. I may encounter a few raised eyebrows when I declare that my *sign* is a metal triangle with the word "Yield" stamped across the middle of it, but it makes painfully perfect sense to me. With all due respect to astrology, this common road sign reveals more about who I am and what the future holds for me than any bull with a car named after him ever could.

I never paid much attention to road signs of any kind until high school, when I got my driver's permit and suddenly became legally accountable for the messages they bore. Almost immediately, I slipped into sign overload. It was nearly impossible to take note of all the do's and don'ts the signs seemed to be screaming at me and still keep my attention on the road. I had always equated being able to drive with liberation and independence, and I was irritated and downright annoyed by these constant reminders that my newfound power was subject to rules and limitations.

It didn't help that I spent my driver-in-training years in a busy suburb of Chicago where cars outnumbered people and getting to any destination was a heart-pounding survival challenge. Highways teetered between raceways and parking lots, and the sheer volume of cars on the road sent me into input overload. It also didn't help that the family car was an over-the-hill Chevy station wagon the size of an aircraft carrier with a manual transmission and a menopausal clutch. Not only was the hideous moss monster difficult to drive, but being spotted in public behind the wheel of that sad excuse for a motor vehicle had an embarrassment factor of twenty on a scale of one to ten.

My loathing for the family car combined with my refusal to take driving lessons from my highly anxious father meant that I completed my senior year in high school and headed off to college without that coveted driver's license.

College, for me, meant four years sequestered in a small town in southern Illinois where the cars-on-campus policy could be summed up in one word: NO. My freshman year, I dated a "townie"—a local boy—mostly because he was a sweet guy with a big heart, but the fact that he had his very own car (a sleek black Buick convertible with a V8 under the hood) added significantly to the chemistry between us. He jumped at the chance to teach me how to drive and, finally, at nineteen, I officially became the legal operator of a motor vehicle.

From the moment I exited the driver's license bureau as a newly anointed pedal-pushing teen driver, I embraced that license as my passport to power. I was ready to take my place on the road to somewhere in what I perceived to be a ruthlessly competitive, winner-takes-all world. When I encountered one of those annoying *Yield* signs, I'd speed up rather than slow down, charging ahead of the oncoming traffic, which would then, of course, have to yield to me. I may have been a danger to both myself and everyone else on the road, but I was absolutely convinced that getting ahead meant getting there *first*.

Seated behind the wheel of a car, tapping into my newly acquired horsepower, I was not only in charge of where I was going, but I could also get there really, really fast by stomping down on the gas pedal. It was all about claiming my power and taking my rightful place as princess of the passing lane. Other drivers, traffic lights, and the seemingly endless stream of road signs I encountered were annoying obstacles that served no purpose other than to slow my progress. My mantra was power, and my definition of that power was absolutely never yielding to anyone or anything. In short, I was the perfect example of someone going nowhere fast, while leaving others in my dust.

Power is an interesting thing, and most of us have a love-hate relationship with it.

We love it when we experience personal power, the power of love, the power within, and so on, because all of these uses empower us. In this setting, power is a good thing.

But at the same time, we hate it when power corrupts or power is abused. Then power is a bad thing. The truth, of course, is that power, in and of itself, is neither good nor bad; its quality depends on how we use it.

My best friend in high school, Arlene, and I were both cursed with the label of "level-headed and responsible," which meant that the adults in our lives trusted us without reservation. It was a heavy burden for two teenage girls struggling to be as rebellious and "normal" as our angst-ridden friends.

Opportunities to exert our power and defy those who would suppress us typically slipped by unused because we were complete cowards when it came to facing the consequences of disobedient acts. Still, we were also teenagers, and where there are teens, drama follows.

It was a simple "parents are out of town and the teenage daughter is left home alone" scenario. Also left at home was the family truck, which my friend's father had expressly forbidden her to drive except in case of emergency.

That emergency arose within an hour of her parents' departure. An urgent call from a classmate, insisting that we come over for an impromptu late afternoon gaggle-of-girls gossip fest, sent us into action. Clever and resourceful as we were, we hatched a foolproof plan to borrow the truck and return it to the exact same location in the garage where we found it. We ingeniously marked the wheel placement with masking tape and prepared to remove the vehicle from its parking place. Although we'd both watched dozens of episodes of *Leave it to Beaver* and *Father Knows Best*, where ill-fated teenage deceptions ended in disaster on a weekly basis, we boldly moved forward with our plan.

While my friend got into the truck and started the engine, I ran to the far right end of the driveway, where I was strategically positioned to keep an eye out for tattle-tale neighbors and then quickly hop into the cab once the vehicle was clear of the garage. Arlene turned on the engine, put the truck in reverse, and slowly began backing up. The radio was up loud enough to drown out a drum and bugle corps, and Arlene was overly focused on not running over the trash cans at the end of the driveway—which may explain why, when she began backing out of the garage, she failed to notice that the right side of her front bumper had gotten caught on the frame of the garage door. As she backed out, she had her head turned sharply to the left so she could check the edge of the driveway and the street behind her, which meant she was totally oblivious to what was happening with the right front bumper. I stood there helplessly as the entire garage door frame began, slowly, to pull away from its moorings as *Do Wah Diddy Diddy* played loudly in the background. Although the total collapse of the frame took less than a minute, every excruciatingly painful second would be etched in my memory for a lifetime.

It played out like an episode from one of those funniest home videos shows: me flailing my arms hysterically, my friend backing out while the radio blared, the door frame ripping itself from the garage opening. . . . It wasn't until the truck finally came to a full stop at the edge of the sidewalk that Arlene noticed the doorframe, which was now mostly detached and teetering on its side in the driveway.

I *almost* burst into that awkward, self-conscious laughter, but the reality of what had just happened set in quickly, and instead, I became mute and motionless, frozen in a shock/panic pose as I witnessed our carefully conceived plan unravel right before my eyes. There was little chance this mishap was going to slip by unnoticed. No matter how carefully we repositioned the truck back in the garage, the significant alteration to the outside of the house was bound to expose our intentions.

When it came to demanding our power, we not only hadn't won the war, we hadn't even made a respectable showing in the battle.

Fortunately, my friend's parents had a lenient punishment policy for first-time offenders and she was only grounded until she raised enough money from babysitting at twenty-five cents an hour to pay for a new garage door, *or* until she turned thirty— whichever came first.

Let's face it: even as adults, getting us to surrender what we perceive to be *our* power to anyone or anything would take a loaded weapon or one of those personal trainers on *The Biggest Loser*. It makes no difference whether the power struggle involves parents, friends, family members, bosses, co-workers, or even people we've never met. We not only resist relinquishing control, but we deny even being able to *see* that *Yield* sign twenty feet in front of us.

Pesky control issues have been a recurring theme in my life. God knows (literally) how much time I've spent trying to force things to happen in a certain way according to a certain timeline that best fit into the fractured-fairytale version of my life story. As a result, my relationship with my spirit has been less than functional.

In my version of the Linda/God relationship, God was some kind of genie who granted me three wishes whenever I needed them, and reloaded my gold "Master(y)" card on a monthly basis.

When I was young, I remember trying to get God to do what I wanted through a variety of different tactics, including, but not limited to, begging, demanding, throwing a tantrum, bargaining, and threatening.

Yes, I did say threatening. When I was eight years old, I told God that unless I got a cocker spaniel puppy for my birthday, I was never going to Sunday school again. I stuffed my black patent leather Sunday shoes into a paper bag and hid them behind the dresser to let God know I was serious. My strategy didn't work. I never got the puppy, my Mom found the shoes during her weekly cleaning, *and* my parents saw to it that I had perfect attendance at church for the next two years.

The truth is: demanding simply doesn't work. That's why beseeching God has rarely gotten us what we wanted. All the "please, pleases" in the world simply won't get us the things we desire if we're not willing to take some responsibility for manifesting our own good.

As it turned out, I was allergic to dogs anyway—so much so that my eyes itched and my nose dripped just watching episodes of *Lassie*. And there was absolutely no room for any pet larger than a ladybug in the overstuffed two-bedroom apartment where we lived. Apparently, God had a better grasp of the big picture than I did. I still threw out the glow-in-the-dark cross I got from Sunday School in protest and refused to be one of the Three Wise Women in that year's Christmas pageant. At that time, I was probably too young to understand what a *Yield* sign meant, even if it had dropped down from my bedroom ceiling in the middle of my bedtime prayers. But I knew that having God on my side was a good thing; I just didn't know how to partner with spirit to co-create the life of my dreams rather than the life of my nightmares.

Along the roadway, a *Yield* sign's purpose is to allow traffic to flow smoothly. When I ignore the warning to yield and force my way into traffic, I impede the progress of every car on the road, including my own. My less-than-desirable consequences have included everything from minor delays to major life interruptions. Experiences like my ill-advised first marriage come to mind. Convinced that if I didn't get my Mrs. within six months of receiving my BA, I was destined to wander the earth for the rest of my days, single, and alone. I took no chances and said "I do" (to a partner that later turned out to be a clear DON'T) within a week after graduating from college. Delay time: twenty-one years.

Or, how about investing and reinvesting in a retail store long after it ceased to be profitable and even longer after it ceased to be fun. Delay time: eight years. (Fifteen years if I factor in the "ceased to be fun" piece.) Oh, and then there was my post-divorce relationship with a man I was determined to turn into a Mr. Right even though everything about that relationship was Mr. Right Now and Mr. So Very Wrong for the long-term. Fortunately, he saved me from myself when he ran off with another woman. Delay time: two years.

Of course, none of these examples were on my list of desired experiences. That's because, in my effort to manipulate outcomes, I failed to yield to that greater perspective I was not able to see from my limited vantage point at the bottom of the trash heap. Everything we desire becomes available to us the moment we stop trying to make it happen. When we manipulate, or push into what we want, we limit God's ability to create something even greater for us. The universe creates from a place of infinite possibility, providing seemingly miraculous solutions to our most impossible problems. When we are willing to go with the flow and release any attachment to how and when things fall into place, life becomes joyful and effortless.

When we have our one-on-one quality time with God, rather than simply passing on a "wants" list ten pages long (with detailed footnotes), we'd be better served by asking for an open heart, good listening skills, and a modicum of wisdom.

We don't need to demand power because we already have it; in fact, we've *always* had it. Just by bringing God into the equation, we automatically become power-full. Everything we do becomes effortless.

Of course, it's easy to yield to God when things are going well. When my business was prosperous, it was easy to joyfully release my business affairs to spirit. I trusted, I yielded, and I expressed gratitude gleefully every time I made a deposit into my golden-ticket bank account that was overflowing with abundance. Things got a little testier, and the skip in my step turned into a limp when business slowed down, sales declined, and invoices weren't getting paid on time. Oh, sure, I still trusted in God, but . . .

A few summers ago, I stopped at a local garage sale and was excited to find a brand new box of affirmation cards for the couldn't-possibly-turn-it-down price of fifty cents. The box contained dozens of life-affirming positive declarations about love, peace, abundance, health, and so on. I was cautiously optimistic about a possible shift in my "luck."

For the next month, before I went to work in the mornings, I shuffled the cards until they felt "right" and then drew one that would become my affirmation for the day. Somehow, I always seemed to pick just the right card at the right time—a clear sign, I felt, that I was getting both important and timely "messages" from God.

One Monday morning, following a particularly aggravating week at work and an exasperating sleep-deprived weekend, I shuffled the cards and reached for an affirmation that I hoped would steer me in a more hopeful direction. The card I picked advised, "Trust the process of life." I took a deep breath, repeated the affirmation several times, and headed off to work. Although I did manage to survive (albeit battered and a little beaten) a very trying day of employees skirmishing with customers and warring with each other, I was having my doubts about how helpful the "Trust the process of life" message had been for me. For the next three days I got up each morning, shuffled the cards, and drew one out, searching for some new insight, some miraculous breakthrough. On each of those three days, I drew the exact same card, "Trust the process of life."

I was beginning to wonder whether I was stuck like Bill Murray in a remake of the movie *Groundhog Day*, where the same events would continue to replay in a seemingly endless loop until I figured out the hidden message. A friend joked that maybe I'd purchased some kind of trick deck with all identical cards. Publicly, I laughed at her suggestion, but privately . . . well, let's just say I may have double-checked the deck a couple of times, just out of curiosity, of course. What I finally realized was that the only trick involved was paying attention to the original message the first time I got it so it didn't need to be repeated all those additional times.

Eventually, I got tired of being hit over the head with the same cosmic two-by-four day after day and succumbed to the wisdom of the cards. Once I actually did that and quit struggling with myself and my employees, things settled down, and the atmosphere at work miraculously shifted from combative to content. People got along with each other, and my job became not only bearable, but pleasant, and effortless. The trust message paid off big time.

Trust is just another word for yield. Every challenge, every opportunity for growth involves surrendering to spirit. Once we put out there what it is we wish to manifest in our lives, we then need to release it to God, no strings attached, no hidden agenda, no unspoken (or spoken) expectations. Until we *do* release it, we continue to spin our wheels, stuck in a rut that grows exponentially larger until it more closely resembles an abandoned gravel pit. It is only in yielding that we can effortlessly get back on the road and comfortably continue the journey forward. Less struggle always results in greater possibility.

Slow: Children at Play

So I bought my inner child a Baby Wet 'N Wail, opened a few cans of Play-Doh®, and finger painted my way through six rolls of white butcher paper. Yet, reconnecting with the child I once was left me flat. All I really reconnected with was my childhood need to take afternoon naps. That's because it's not about watching reruns of Sesame Street or swinging in those child-sized sling seats till your tush goes numb.

Where was the girl who giggled 'til she dropped or who could double-dutch like there was no tomorrow, or offer up to her diary her innermost thoughts on coconut Good Humor® bars?

Alas, she is stretched out on the La-Z-Boy®, watching the season finale of Desperate Housewives, while half-heartedly journaling in a dog-eared spiral-bound notebook with the cast of High School Musical 3 on the cover. A body (or mind) in motion stays in motion—when did mine decide to park itself in an overstuffed piece of furniture with a three-speed vibrator? And when did I trade in my joy of living for a remote control?

My inner child ran away from home sometime during puberty! It's taken decades to discover just how much she took with her. What I miss most is how she would joyfully free-fall from one experience to the next without fear, trusting herself because she trusted in spirit first. I miss how she would dive into wild abandoned dance at the first sound of music; race through backyard alley ways just to feel the wind on her face and arms; cardboard slide down grassy hills; skip through the hallways with one hand reaching for the wall; cartwheel spontaneously in a dress; and practice twirling a baton on her walk home from school. Unconcerned was I about any twists or turns in my road ahead. Then, I simply took to the road for the play in the journey.

The essence of a beautiful, nurturing childhood grows and flourishes with the freedom of knowing that your life is unfolding in a manner that allows you the greatest growth, awareness, and consciousness.

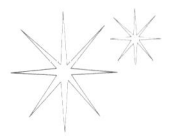

CHAPTER
9

When I was five years old, I developed my first movie star crush. I fell hopelessly, head-over-heels-in love with the heroic leading man-boy in Walt Disney's *Peter Pan*. Every evening, I would pull back my hair into a curly ponytail held in place with a large, blue satin bow (just like the "real" Wendy), don my official (ninety percent nylon chiffon and ten percent magic dust) sky blue Wendy nightgown with puffy sleeves and satin ribbon waistband, and wait on the window seat for my pixie prince to come.

Never mind that he was little more than ink and celluloid, I still spent endless hours staring out the window of my bedroom, scanning the skies for a cute little red-headed boy in a green Christmas elf costume who flew as though he had wings, leaving a contrail of twinkling stars in his wake.

The object of my affection was the perfect male. He was impishly handsome, adventurous, brave, chivalrous, kind, compassionate, and caring. And, of course, he also knew how to fly (and was willing to share with others his gravity-defying secret). But even more importantly, he had unlimited access to Neverland—the place where no one had to grow up and anyone's childhood could be preserved for eternity. Neverland was the realm of possibility and living there meant no boundaries, no limitations, no alarm clocks, and no chasing time. The only clock in Neverland was the one inside the Crocodile and it was focused exclusively on Captain Hook.

Neverland wasn't without danger, however. There were pirates, lost boys, and a jealous fairy to deal with, for starters. And then, of course, there was the infamous plank incident, but somehow it all worked out in the end. You knew the good guys would always win because they lived in the Neverland reality of happy endings.

I, like Wendy, never forgot Peter, even as the decades rolled by. As an adult, I was distracted, but only temporarily, by a few Peter Pan wannabees—men who just didn't want to grow up . . . period—but nothing could cause me to betray the magical memories of the boy who held the key to the long-locked door to my childhood.

I even promised Peter, as I slipped the storybook recounting his adventures into a plain brown box headed for storage, that I would name my first child after him. In college, I related my sacred promise to my roommate, who was so moved she took the vow with me, agreeing to dub her first born "Peter" as well.

(When she got serious with a guy whose last name was Piper, however, she begged to be let out of her obligation.)

My first child was a daughter, and because she was so "darling," I seriously considered calling her Wendy, but her father wasn't buying the whole Peter Pan thing, which meant my alternate suggestion to name her "Tinkerbell" didn't fly either.

Ironically, when I finally did have a son, I was forced to abandon *my* vow as well, because, alas, his last name would be Abbott and Peter Abbott rolled off the tongue in such a way that it would have sounded more like a bow to Beatrice Potter than James Barrie. (We plan, God laughs.) Naming my son after an animated film star probably wasn't the best way to go about holding on to some remnant of my childhood, anyway.

There's something in us, even at age five, that knows our time as a kid is pretty special, and keeping it safe and sacred is the key to thriving (rather than just surviving) as an adult. Aging is inevitable, but leaving that child within behind us, as we grow into adulthood, is a conscious choice. It's what I would call "inner child neglect." It's punishable by a lifetime of frustrating adult ills, such as, but not limited to:

Repeated Failure Syndrome
Dead Ends Disease
Flailing Relationships Flu

There aren't any magic formulas for reconnecting with the child within, but there are some strategies that work better than others. Redefining time is a good place to start. In case you haven't noticed, time only chases adults (see Captain Hook example above)—time never runs out for kids—there's always plenty of it. That's the part of the "never" in Neverland that often gets missed. If time *never* runs out, there's no hurry to grow up and accomplish a bunch of things that will impress our family and friends. We also don't need to fret over where we're "going" because we'll always be in the here and now. Kids get that.

When it came time for my first born to start kindergarten, I struggled with whether I should drive her to school or allow her to walk those seven long blocks by herself. I remembered having to walk much farther than that when I started school (but, of course, not nearly as far as my mother, who trudged through miles of snow, her fingers turning blue as she clutched the tear-stained pages of her homework to her breast, etc., etc.). A little adversity builds character, after all, and walking seven blocks (even in the rain and snow) would be good for Dawn in the long run.

It wasn't an easy decision. I was shunned by the other parents in the neighborhood, who loaded their precious little five-year-olds into their station wagons each morning and delivered them refreshed, dry, and safe to the front door of the elementary school. Guilt, along with their disapproving looks and hushed conversations whenever I came within earshot, *almost* got to me, and I reluctantly agreed to drive her for the first few days. But after that, I insisted, she would be on her own. After all, I still had her three-year-old sister to attend to, *and* I was six months pregnant—well past the mother-to-be "glow" stage. I was determined to find some way to get my daughter to school safely without having to provide wheeled delivery service.

So when I discovered that one of her classmates who lived nearby was making the daily walk to school, I immediately contacted Sara's mother and made arrangements for the two girls to go together. It seemed like the perfect solution. The girls would be walking buddies and could keep a watchful eye on each other.

It worked perfectly . . . for about a week. Then I got the phone call from her school that every parent dreads getting—the one they reenact on those investigative news shows that have a penchant for spotlighting nightmarish kidnapping cases. The school secretary was doing her best to keep the tone light and upbeat, but the cracking in her voice betrayed her attempt at nonchalance. After some polite conversation about the weather, she got to the point. It was 10:00 a.m., a full hour after the starting bell had rung, and the girls had not arrived at school!

I made a couple of quick emergency phone calls, frantically herded my half-dressed toddler into the car, and set off in a panic to find my lost daughter and her companion *before* we became headline news. I backed out of the garage at full speed, tires screeching, put the car in drive, and gunned it to the end of the block where I took the corner at twice the posted speed. Less than 100 feet down the next block, I slammed on the brakes, and brought the car squealing to an abrupt stop. There, in plain sight, were the two five-year-olds, seated on the curb (their school packs tossed onto the sidewalk behind them) floating dried leaves and twigs down the water-filled gutter next to the road. They greeted me with big smiles and muddy hands, blissfully unaware of the 60 Minutes news crew speeding towards our home. They proudly showed me their fleet of aspen leaf boats and invited me to sail with them. Neither of the girls seemed to comprehend why I was hyperventilating and making screeching sounds as I spoke. They assured me that they were making their way to school—one block at a time. This block, they had discovered, had an impromptu river to navigate; who knew what lovely surprises the next block would reveal.

What was the big hurry anyway? Good question. Yes, the girls needed to learn to get to school on time, but was that really what this was all about? It was hard to be angry with them. Who was I to say that learning the numbers between one and twenty was more important than engineering seaworthy ships out of fallen leaves? Or imagining an entire armada on its way to some distant land? Or finding joy in play time?

Slowing down and taking time to play is the lesson children have for us. Play is important. As kids, we know it intuitively; as adults, we deny what we've known for eternity.

Slow: Children at Play is one of those signs that demands we take our foot off the gas pedal—at least for the next few blocks. What if it were also an invitation to take a break, seek out a child who can remind us *how* to play, and spend some quality totally-in-the-moment "now" time?

Whenever I crashed and burned for the fourth time in as many weeks, I'd call my now adult daughter and schedule some time with my favorite Zen master—my little grandson, Aidan. Babies don't care about networking luncheons, text messaging, or dust-free houses with sparkling clean floors. They react to vibrating Blackberries with little more than mild curiosity, and they think laundry is something to wear on your head. The TV's remote control is often more interesting than the television itself, and the main motivation for learning to crawl is to finally be able to examine the dog's dish, up close and personal. They can erase your worries with the flash of a smile and engage you in a marathon game of peek-a-boo that renders time meaningless.

I remember many hours of sitting on the lawn with my grandson, watching him pull up one fistful of grass after another. With the freshly-picked greens oozing through his fingers, he would raise his hand as high as he could, open his fist, and watch the crumpled blades float gently back to the ground. Oblivious to everything else going on around him, he repeated this little ritual again and again, giggling each and every time in joyful anticipation as he released his bounty onto the breeze. Spending time with this precious child taught me more about living consciously than my entire library of spiritual teachings. I learned that I could always count on the wisdom of the Aidans in our world.

I've come to believe that the time we should have spent slowing down and playing (but didn't) is actually taken from us as some form of cosmic scolding. The harder I work, the less I get done. The more I play, the more relaxed I become, and the more I get done. Why exactly that is, I'm not sure, but I suspect it's related to the "Too Stressed to be Blessed" principle, which can be summed up in one concise bumper sticker: "Ask not for whom the clock ticks: it ticks for thee." (Captain Cook had that one plastered across the stern of his ship.) However, the clock only ticks for thee if you plug it in or provide it with batteries. It needs energy to operate; if we don't give it any of ours, it stops. Hence the phrase: time stands still.

I recently had an opportunity to not only stop time, but send it backwards, via a blast from the past experience with a couple hundred old photos of my life and times in the Midwest. Even though I spent most of my middle school years only a couple of miles from Chicago's legendary Riverview Park, I had only two slightly blurred pictures documenting those wild, crazy, adrenaline-rush days at the fun-never-stops amusement park.

The bulk of the photos portrayed me and my younger siblings enjoying clearly Kodak-happy moments at the modest, no-frills playground across the street from where I lived from birth to age eleven.

There I was, in full black-and-white, gleefully pushing my brother on the swings; there I was doing a balancing act with my much younger twin sisters, who were teetering tandem while I tottered. There I was perched atop the monkey bars, posing as queen of the jungle; there I was covered in sand, laying the foundation for what would become a sand castle fit for a queen (of the jungle). There I was performing daredevil, upside down, head-first moves down the silver slide; and finally, there I was clinging to the bars as half the kids on the playground spun me around in the child-powered merry-go-round.

In a particularly ah-filled moment, as warm fuzzy memories came flooding back in, I began to think about how I should create one of those "All I Really Need to Know I Learned in Kindergarten"* type posters and just substitute *playground*.

Under the "All I Need to Know . . ." heading, I would list all of my favorite playground equipment, followed by a short interpretation of its metaphorical meaning. And if it's clever enough, it could even end up as a bookmark of something.

Teeter Totter

A good play-full relationship is one that is balanced.

You can't teeter without a totter, but pick your totter carefully or you may find yourself up in the air with no way to get down.

Monkey Bars

Gravity works. If you want to be a climber, you have to love to fall.

Learning how to climb means you're never stuck at the bottom. But occasionally, ending up there is part of the learning curve.

---

*Robert Fulghum, *All I Really Need to Know I Learned in Kindergarten*, 1986, Ballantine Books.

Swings

How high you can go often depends on how hard someone pushes you.

You can take a swing pretty high all by yourself, but you can get there faster if you're not afraid to ask for a push.

Merry-go-round

When you find yourself going around in circles, it's really important to hold on tight.

Going around and around and around and around *always* ends up being a dizzying experience. It's important to think about that before you begin the ride.

Slide

Life is filled with ups and downs, but you can always turn the downs into ups.

Using the stairs is the only accepted way to go up a slide. But going down? There are lots of options—face first, feet first, sunny side up, over easy, or freestyle. Life is more fun when you enjoy all aspects of every experience.

Sandbox

Sandcastles aren't subject to building codes.

There are no rules to building a sandcastle, so dig right in. If you're not covered in sand by the time you're done, you haven't truly embraced the experience. But don't get too attached to your masterpiece. It can be washed away in the crash of a wave. Simply know that you can build again and again. Creativity has no limits.

Who knew the playground across the street from my house held so much wisdom? A child could have told me if I'd been there to listen. There's a reason why there are benches in a playground: it's a place for adults to sit and observe the children.

Author Eric Hoffer wrote, "It is the child in the man that is the source of his uniqueness and creativeness, and the playground is the optimal milieu for the unfolding of his capacities and talents."

How do we relearn how to play? Play has a purpose. It allows us to relax, have fun, quit taking ourselves so seriously, giggle, laugh, and be creative. There is no right or wrong in play—just joy.

Access to Neverland is gained through the mind of a child—any child—not just those named Peter. That mind can also exist in adults if we first create the space and TIME for it and, secondly, keep it healthy with regular doses of silliness, fantasy, creativity, and play. You can't fake Neverland, (even if you're a celebrity) by building an amusement park in your back yard and spending a lot of time on the Ferris wheel. It's a million dollar state of mind, but it can't be purchased at any price—it must be consciously created.

You can start by hanging a "Do Not Disturb—I'm at Play" sign on the door to your office, garage, or laundry room . . . wherever you spend most of your time. Make sure everyone knows you mean it, including yourself. Then make a commitment to spend the day enjoying every moment. Take breaks, laugh out loud for no reason, or create a sculpture out of paper clips—whatever it takes to remind yourself that the world really is your playground, swings have a higher purpose than dealing with moods, and Neverland is a place you *never* have to leave.

Caution: Low Flying Aircraft

I was driving along a snow-packed, rural state highway that bordered a small airport when I saw my first one. It was a curious sign that warned, in a most matter-of-fact manner: *Caution: Low Flying Aircraft.* Really? As my fertile imagination began envisioning planes scraping the roofs of cars with their landing gear, my initial puzzlement turned to stomach-churning apprehension. (It didn't help that I already had a disturbingly long list of issues with planes. . . .) Were they serious? Cars on this highway had to not only watch out for other drivers, dazed and confused wildlife, and the occasional runaway family pet, but we now had to be prepared to dodge airplanes coming in for a landing?

Holy Amelia Earhart, I thought, just how low do these planes fly? Would they buzz my car just for the fun of it? Would the exhaust fumes overwhelm the pine needle-scented pomander I had dangling from the rear view mirror? Did I need to close up the top on my Mustang convertible if I wanted to preserve my leather upholstery?

How could aircraft be a hazard for motorists, I wondered? My husband's nephew once had to land an airplane on a busy interstate, but surely that wasn't typical along this stretch of road, was it? Was the landing strip so short that planes might be backed up in the turning lane?

After gathering my wits about me and reeling in my runaway thoughts, I realized that I should actually be grateful for that helpful sign. If it hadn't been so thoughtfully placed on the side of the road, I might have been startled by that plane swooping down to within a few feet of the top of my head and lose control of my car. But now, with this warning, I can just take a deep breath and simply wave at the pilot as he whizzes by.

In reality, we don't often get advance warning about airborne objects that could prove to be a danger to our well being. These low flying aircraft (LFAs) are a serious cause for concern. Forget UFOs; there's a "new" and far more immediate threat than some aliens with a faulty GPS. (I'll worry about them when they get around to posting a sign.)

LFAs can prove to be a danger to yourself and others, especially if you're one of them. The human version of an LFA is someone who has experienced failure and is afraid of flying higher than where they can safely jump out and evacuate.

It takes courage to fly. Failure grounds you, dooms you to life as a flight **un**-worthy LFA. Allowing other low flying aircraft to buzz you is no better. (Wallowing in someone else's misery can be at least as detrimental to your happiness as sloshing around in your own.)

Flying so close to the ground means we never experience the thrill of soaring. If we allow our fear of failure to dictate whether or not we aspire to higher experiences, we'll never even get off the ground.

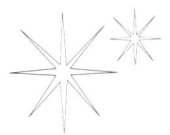
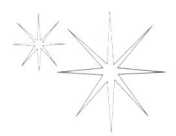

CHAPTER
10

In my mid-twenties, I suddenly developed a fear of flying. It was actually more than just a fear. The thought of getting into an airplane triggered a feeling of terror that would have given Rambo pause. It was unmatched by anything I'd ever experienced.

I'd only logged a handful of air miles prior to my first attack of flight-induced panic at age twenty-two. I hadn't even *seen* the inside of a real airplane, much less ridden in one, before I was in high school. My dad played the poverty card every time the subject of air travel came up. "Our family's too big and our income's too small for us to be taking expensive airplane trips," he would say. No further discussion was ever allowed.

My mother, who saw flying as both convenient and blissfully indulgent, fantasized about financial windfalls that would magically transform us into jet setters, circling the globe from 30,000 feet up. However, no matter how much she pleaded, begged, or cried, my father stuck to his plan "to see the USA in our Chevrolet." If it was good enough for Dinah Shore, it was good enough for us. As a result, I associated air travel with monetary stress and emotional meltdowns. I wasn't in any particular hurry to start accumulating flight miles.

I took my first airplane trip when I was sixteen—a short flight from Chicago to Springfield, Illinois. A local radio station had sponsored a writing contest on "How Broadcasters Serve the Nation," and the six-line poem I crafted during a "mental health" day off from high school was chosen for the top prize. My reward was $500, a flight on a small commuter jet to the state capitol, lunch with the then Governor Otto Kerner, and the opportunity to read my prize-winning piece to the attendees at the National Broadcaster's Convention.

Even *before* the standing ovation (I was still too young and naïve to realize that roaring applause was pretty much obligatory in these situations), I was "flying high," and I knew my no-stopping-me-now future was written in the fluffy white clouds beneath the wings of that marvelous airplane that had safely delivered me to my date with destiny. The VIP trip to Springfield was the gift that kept on giving. I did radio interviews, was featured in local newspaper articles, and enjoyed a couple of months of celebrity status with my peers back at Forest View High School.

Several years passed before I had another opportunity to fly. In the interim, I'd graduated from college, gotten married, and finished graduate school. My second flight was a trip on a commercial airline to Rochester, New York, where my then-husband and I would be living while he was training for a newly acquired position with a large company.

With a first-class ticket that had been bestowed upon me by his generous employer, I was perfectly poised to begin my next great adventure. As the plane took off from Denver, I sat back and smiled the smile of a pampered princess. I spent the flight sipping champagne while luxuriating in the roomy leather seats. Life was good. I made a connection in Pittsburgh and caught the short flight to Rochester. This second plane was much smaller; passengers were packed in tightly; and even in first class, I kept rubbing shoulders with my uncomfortably-close row mate.

I once again enjoyed the rush of the takeoff, focused on the fading landscape below, and decided to make the best of the crowded quarters. The businessman next to me initiated some light conversation, the stewardess kept me supplied with cans of Fresca and packages of salted nuts, and the time passed quickly. As the plane began its descent, I noticed that I was beginning to feel light-headed and, in spite of the two sticks of gum I was chewing vigorously, the pressure in my ears was mounting. I could feel a buzzing sensation in my head, and both the sights and sounds around me became fuzzy and blurred. Noises seemed far away, and people's voices sounded like distant echoes in a long tunnel. Something was definitely wrong. A piercing pain in my left ear quickly overwhelmed my other senses, and within seconds, everything went black.

I don't know how much time passed (undoubtedly only a minute or two), but as I regained consciousness, I slowly became aware of a flurry of activity taking place around me. Apparently, my blackout had not gone unnoticed. The man seated next to me was now standing in the aisle, waving his hands frantically, trying to attract the attention of a flight attendant. The two women from across the aisle were hovering over me, one propping my head up with a pillow while the other tried to get me to drink some water. The people in the row ahead of me were turned around, peering over the back of their seats, curious about the drama that was unfolding behind them. The pain in my ear was now eclipsed by the sudden rush of blood to my face, the feeling that I was about to die of embarrassment, and a growing concern that somebody might be recording this event for posterity (or the insurance company).

Upon landing, I was ceremoniously escorted off the plane (even *more* mortifying) by the airport's emergency personnel and delivered to my husband. We left the airport and drove directly to a local doctor who declared, rather matter-of-factly, that I had ruptured an eardrum. The plane's descent into Rochester was sharper and more rapid than I'd been able to tolerate. Going up had been easy; coming down had been brutal.

It was almost two years before I found the courage to give flying another try.

Accompanied by my husband and six-month-old daughter, I boarded a flight to Chicago, where we planned to celebrate the baby's first Christmas. Despite reassurances from both my doctor *and* my husband that a repeat of the Rochester experience was highly unlikely, I spent most of the flight white-knuckled and clinging to the armrest. The descent into Chicago went without incident, yet I rushed out of the plane hardly able to breathe. Getting me on that return flight to Denver several days later took three hours of coaxing from my husband, a Valium, and the promise of two Bloody Marys before takeoff. I spent most of the flight alternating between hyperventilating and weeping uncontrollably. Thankfully, the landing in Denver was near perfect, but I still all but vaulted over several rows of passengers in a panicked attempt to get off the plane as quickly as possible. It would be more than twenty years before I flew again. The memory of one painful descent dictated what my life would look like for two decades.

It took a great deal of effort to avoid flying, particularly since I was determined to keep my illogical fear of airplanes a secret from friends and family as long as possible. For starters, I had to become proficient at lying: " Mom, of course I'd love to go with you to Europe. Unfortunately, I've been asked to take over a colleague's classes while he undergoes quadruple bypass surgery . . . or double hip replacement . . . I can't remember exactly, but I just can't do it."

I became masterful at making up excuses: "Honey, you know I'd love to join you on that business trip to Atlanta, but leaving the kids that long with a babysitter would be traumatic for them, or maybe me. I just can't do that to them/me/us."

I learned how to play the illness card: "Of course I'd like to fly back to Chicago for the reunion, but my asthma has been acting up and it *is* the height of allergy season. You wouldn't want me to go into anaphylactic shock during the middle of the Remember When Luncheon, would you?"

I severely restricted vacation travel to locations we could access by car: "No, I don't really want to go to Hawaii. I'm not all that into warm breezes, sandy beaches, and piña coladas. Besides, I think a camping trip to a nearby state park would help the kids better appreciate what we have right here in our own backyard."

It was easier to become an expert in the art of deception than it was to face my fear of flying. I spent most of my time ducking and dodging in order to avoid being buzzed by the low flying aircraft I had become.

It wasn't as if I didn't *try* to gain altitude. I read every fear-of-flying self-help book I could get my hands on and dutifully scheduled sessions with kindly psychotherapists. I was told that what I was experiencing was considered a garden-variety phobia and no big deal. It was a big deal to me.

My grandmother, the quintessential nervous flyer, would have understood. She was willing to endure any amount of inconvenience necessary to avoid what she deemed as the unfriendly skies.

However, once a year, she would gather up her courage, throw a bottle of tranquilizers into her purse, and board a plane for the fifteen-hundred-mile trip from Florida to Chicago to visit her family. Although I wasn't usually part of the kiss-and-hug welcoming committee that greeted her upon arrival, I was allowed to tag along when it came time to take Grandma back to O'Hare for her return trip home.

While we unloaded her bags from the back of the station wagon, Grandma would throw her carpetbag-size patent leather purse over her shoulder, scurry into the terminal, and head straight for the coin-operated "Airline Trip Insurance" vending machine where she would purchase $50,000 worth of coverage.

My grandmother was absolutely convinced that riding in an airplane was a death-defying undertaking and she was willing to back up that belief with a coin purse full of quarters. She'd invest a couple of dollars every time she flew to be absolutely sure that if, indeed, that plane went down with her aboard, someone would be held accountable. Her plane never went down, and the insurance company made a little money off one more passenger with more cash than confidence.

Fear of flying, both literally and figuratively, is a learned skill. You know you've mastered it when you can calculate the twenty-two ways something can go wrong in a given situation even before you've had time to consider even one way in which it might go right. Some fear, of course, is necessary to survive. However, when that fear escalates to include anything and everything outside our comfort zone—and that comfort zone keeps shrinking in size—we suddenly find ourselves earthbound for life. We begin to methodically avoid new or different experiences, and flying often becomes one of them. Whether we are literally afraid to get on an airplane, or just generally fearful of allowing ourselves to take flights of the spirit, the consequences are equally debilitating.

When my son was little, he was obsessed with Superman. It was my fault. When he was only two years old, I bought him those cute Superman Underoos, added a pair of his sisters' red tights and a makeshift cape, and took him to see his first Superman movie.

Only a few minutes into the film, it was already clear that Derek was destined to become a Super fan. He never touched his popcorn, he remained fixed in his seat for over two hours, and he didn't even notice when his sister pulled on his cape and spilled a box of Good & Plenty® in his lap. During the twenty minute ride home, he chattered nonstop—Suuuperman this, Suuuperman that. When bedtime arrived several hours later, he was still running through the house excitedly, making whooshing sounds as loudly as he could as he flew down the hallway on his way to intercept some unsuspecting ne'er-do-well. Sleep was clearly the furthest thing from his mind, and negotiations to get him into bed included allowing him to spend the night in his Superman outfit. Little did I know what I was agreeing to.

For the next year, he would wear nothing else to bed . . . or anywhere else for that matter. I had to peel him out of his costume while he was sleeping, wash it secretly in my own Fortress of Solitude (the laundry room), and re-dress him before he woke the next morning.

Wherever I went, Superman accompanied me. Superman shopped with me at the grocery store. Superman shared French fries with me at McDonald's®. Superman sat next to me in church on Easter Sunday. And everywhere we went, we got there faster than a speeding bullet because we flew. (To be fair to my son, I walked, and Superman flew.) When necessary, I ran to keep up with the toddler wonder. At home, he was able to leap tall couches with a single bound and he flew past me in the hallway several times during the day on the way to his next mission.

Although he loved everything about his costume—and the persona it allowed him to take on—it was the red cape that he treasured most. His superpowers were in the cape; take it away and he would curl up into a little ball on the floor, claiming he'd been exposed to Kryptonite. It was all about the flying.

It didn't bother him that he never actually got more than a foot or two off the ground and didn't sustain flight for more than a couple of seconds. Sure, he may have started out as low flying aircraft, but he knew it was only the beginning. In his boundless imagination, he was already soaring with eagles, racing jet planes, and circling the globe on a daily basis. Regardless of appearances, he knew in his heart that he was flying at record-breaking altitudes, and no one was going to convince him otherwise.

A friend who had come to know my son the flying phenomenon informed me that, according to comic hero history, Superman's ability to fly was a power added to his repertoire well after his original introduction. Initially, he was merely able to leap great distances, keeping him earthbound for the early part of his comic book career. Yet it was his unique ability to fly that ultimately became his claim to fame. With one giant leap of faith, literally, he discovered (over time) that he could become airborne at will. I'd love to know what popped into that little balloon graphic above his head as he processed making that historic transition. Surely it took some getting used to—even for Superman.

Committing to flight is not always easy. There can be rough weather ahead, or, at the very least, a little airsickness. Flying does not come naturally for us wingless bipeds with all-too-rational minds. So much can go wrong during takeoff and landing, not to mention the seemingly endless list of possible mishaps during the flight itself. Let's face it: when we fly, we're operating without a safety net at the mercy of a pilot we've never actually met in a plane we didn't build.

Even if we're willing to chance the takeoff, after the initial rush of excitement is over, we're faced with a long period of just hanging in the air. If the occasional episodes of annoying turbulence don't get to us, our racing brain does; it begins contemplating the law of gravity and the odds of hundreds of people being able to get safely through a couple of small exit doors in case of a crash. So we begin the downward spiral into fear. Maybe we shouldn't have tried to fly in the first place. What were we thinking? Doubts and more doubts begin to surface. Is it really possible to continue to fly forever? Eventually we have to come down, don't we? What will that experience be like? Is a smooth landing guaranteed and, if not, can we survive a rough touchdown?

Midway through my son's year-long fascination with everything Superman, he discovered a television show called *The Greatest American Hero*. The main character was the quintessential everyman who had the unique opportunity to perform superhero feats on a weekly basis. The show's premise was a little far-fetched, but no one ever claimed it was a reality series.

You had to buy into the premise that genial high-school teacher Ralph Hinkley finds himself in the wrong place at the wrong time and has a close encounter with some friendly little green men. Then you had to go along with the idea that the aliens gifted him with a red suit that seems to give him superpowers. To further challenge your suspension of disbelief, Ralph loses the suit's instruction book and with it, the information he needs to access its special features. So, alas, his success or failure as a superhero becomes dependent on both his problem-solving abilities and his willingness to take risks. In short, although he manages to fly and perform acts of superhuman strength, at least occasionally, he also spends a lot of his in-air time crashing . . . into everything from brick walls to trash cans.

At first, I was a little concerned that my young, impressionable superhero-in-training would be at least mildly traumatized by the endless progression of scenes depicting all the possible ways someone can fail, and fail badly.

However, Derek wasn't the least bit disturbed by Ralph's lackluster success record. Instead, the determined mini-hero threw himself wholeheartedly into spontaneous reenactments of Ralph's most spectacular smashups.

He thought it was fun. He would streak through the house, yelling some unintelligible superhero tag line, and plow head-on into the cushy, oversized, beanbag chair in the family room. At least it wasn't the wall. In spite of Ralph's dubious track record as a flying hero, Derek embraced this new character with wild abandon. He now not only flew everywhere that he went; he also crashed (safely) everywhere he went as well.

He learned to adapt to the highs and lows of the superhero lifestyle without skipping a beat. He crashed, picked himself up, brushed himself off, and lived to fly another day. In his own way, he was training to be fearless.

Of course, it's a lot easier to embrace flying when you're three years old than it is when you're forty. Nobody has yet told you that you can't do it, nobody has cluttered your mind with the pesky details about what it takes to complete a successful flight, and nobody has bothered you with the principles of gravity. Nobody has told you that superhero suits don't work, even if you do have the instructions. Nobody has taught you about failure.

The leap of faith necessary for us to fly doesn't come easily. Our flight journal is often filled with far more fiery crash landings than glorious, breathtaking rides. We've lost faith in ourselves and our ability to succeed. Even when we gather up our courage and convince ourselves that it wouldn't hurt to try *one* more time, far too often, somewhere between takeoff and landing, things begin to go wrong and we abort the flight, sending the plane back to the hangar indefinitely.

"Sure, I'd like to start my own business, but in this economy, it would be suicide!"

"I suppose I could go back to school and finally get the nursing degree I always wanted, but it would take too much time away from my family."

"I'd love to work as a writer, but there's no money in it, and I have to eat!"

The list goes on. We make up all sorts of stuff to avoid having to admit that the real issue is fear of failure.

This kind of fear-based reasoning is exactly the type of crazy rationalizing I did years ago to keep myself as far away from airports as possible.

It wasn't until my daughter Nicole got married and moved twelve hundred miles away that I finally found sufficient motivation to push past my anxiety and get back on an airplane.

My first step was to schedule a business meeting in Chicago and book a "test" flight. I was terrified, but determined. The day before the trip, I developed sudden, excruciating neck pain. My fear was so intense that it was manifesting in my physical body as pain. My husband, trying to lighten my mood, quipped that I looked like a toy robot in need of fresh batteries as I shuffled about the house in slow motion, unable to move my head in any direction.

After two hours of unsuccessful attempts at making me comfortable, i.e., heating pads, followed by ice packs, followed by fudge brownies, followed by heating pads, followed by ice packs, and so on, Bob packed me into the car and drove me to the local hospital. The Emergency Room doctor prescribed a heavy dose of muscle relaxants and strongly recommended (exactly as my fear had scripted it) that I cancel my travel plans. I was in no condition to fly, she said; it would only make things worse. Events were unfolding exactly as "planned." I was already mentally crafting my "regrets" e-mail: "I'm really sorry, but I won't be able to make the meeting. I injured my neck and am completely immobilized. . . ."

It was the even more painful realization that I would remain unable to move—literally—until I did something to break the panic cycle, that gave me an unexpected burst of courage. I did something that would have made my Superboy son proud. Frozen with fear, in a degree of pain that made labor seem like a fond, albeit slightly uncomfortable, memory, groggy from medication, tightly velcroed into a neck brace, and feeling anything *but* heroic, I boarded the plane in Denver. The two-hour flight to Chicago was nothing short of miserable, but I survived it. There was no victory celebration; it took both my husband and a compassionate flight attendant almost 20 minutes to get me off the plane without further trauma, but I had landed safely. Less than two hours after checking into our hotel, a "miracle" rivaling that of turning water into wine occurred—the pain completely disappeared and I was jumping on the king size bed as though nothing had ever happened. I had taken off, flown, and landed—and I was okay. The stiff neck no longer served any purpose and the pain left my body as quickly as it had come.

I now actually enjoy (almost) flying and look forward to vacations beyond Colorado borders, visits with family, and oh-what-the-heck-why-not weekends away. My flights have been blissfully uneventful, with simple, smooth landings.

The moral of the story? On a spiritual level, when we attempt to fly, we often have no idea what heights we'll be able to reach, how comfortable the journey is going to be, or how long we'll be able to remain aloft.

Landings aren't just about what goes up must come down. Every landing is one more step along our path. Rough landings result in delays along the path; obstacles appear, real or imagined, and forward progress is virtually impossible. And those devastating dark nights of the soul? They're essentially crash landings that leave us battered and bruised, but don't have to ground us permanently.

It requires faith to take off, a deep knowing to remain aloft, and wisdom to nail a perfect landing. We trust; we fly; we process what we've learned. Then we repeat it all again. Like any other educational endeavor, getting through flight school successfully takes time and patience.

Over time, the rocky landings become less and less disabling. We also begin to see the laws of gravity from a new perspective; even though what goes up may come down, we have the ability to send ourselves back up again . . . and again . . . if we choose.

My son is now an adult. He got over his fascination with Superman by the time he was in first grade. When he was eight, a psychic told him he was an ancient astronaut who would return to the sky some day. He shrugged his shoulders, smiled, and said, "Of course I am," and walked away, totally unimpressed by her supposed revelation. In junior high, he talked about becoming a 21st century astronaut, but his flight path lead him, instead, to a career as a mechanical engineer, working in the aerospace industry. His fantasy is to retire early and spend the rest of his life traveling, racking up millions of airline miles, and enjoying every one of them.

Flying of the spiritual kind is always free. We come into this incarnation with a prepaid frequent flyer account and unlimited miles. The goal is to actually *use* those miles to get to where we want to go. And in using them, it becomes easier and easier to not only discover where that *is* exactly, but also to plot the most empowering course to get there.

Beware of Dog

I've never actually owned a dog. Growing up, my dad had a strict "no dogs allowed policy" that was put in place long before it was discovered that I was allergic to anything that growled, yipped, or purred, which of course included dogs. My kids were equally deprived. Even if I was willing to live my life in a Benadryl fog in order to provide my children with the pet of their dreams, I still felt that caring for three kids, a husband, a tank full of fish, a couple of outdoor rabbits, and an occasional gerbil that "Not Me" smuggled into the house was already beyond the call of duty.

Besides, whenever I encountered one (or more) canine pets at a friend or family member's home, they barked excitedly at me as if I were a long lost relative, leaped into my lap so they could lick my face, and stared through me as though they knew my every dysfunctional thought and planned on sharing them with my psychiatrist. It was disconcerting. I didn't need to be accountable to anybody else in my life, whether they had two feet or four.

My kids didn't agree with my decision to ban dogs from our home, but I held fast. I bought each of them an oversized stuffed Snoopy, a plastic dog dish, and a sack full of rubber squeak toys and told them to make do.

"But, Mom," my son would plead, "they're the friendly, faithful, all-American pet, loved by many and disliked by only a shunned few."

One of his sisters would then chime in with, "They're lovable, loyal, smart, resourceful, and they will do just about anything for you." For supporting evidence, they would remind me of all those dog heroes (of my era) who had changed the course of history, becoming legends in their own time. I would listen patiently as they recounted how Lassie was a one-dog search and rescue team, Roy Rogers' faithful Bullet the Wonder Dog tackled the bad guys to the ground before Roy even got the gun out of his holster, and how Dick and Jane's faithful dog, Spot, helped stamp out illiteracy in America.

Toto alerted Dorothy's friends when she was being held captive by the Wicked Witch, and then went on to expose the great and powerful wizard as the fraud of Oz. Tramp arranged a noodlelicious candlelight dinner for his Lady on a beggar's budget, and Benji's heroic efforts earned him five movies, four prime-time television specials, and one series.

So who coined the phrase "Beware of Dog" and then made a fortune in the sign business churning out thousands of these warnings each year? Unless you're the embittered sister of the Wicked Witch, what could you possibly have to fear from these cuddly canines?

Well, I suppose it depends on how you look at it. Their public displays of affection are embarrassing, their choice of friends is nondiscriminatory, and their fondness for reconnecting with their inner puppy is downright disturbing. They are overly eager to get to know you, they are willing to do most anything for your time and attention, and they are apparently capable of a degree of unconditional love and devotion that is beyond most people's level of understanding, including mine. So yes, if I'm being honest, they do (or at least did) frighten me. Even the most benign little Yorkie triggered rampant insecurities. A family intervention, which included a *Lassie* marathon and a 2 a.m. viewing of *Old Yeller*, eventually turned things around for me when it came to my fear of dogs, but it was only the tip of a very large and treacherously deep iceberg.

I had a long list of Be-Warys that was growing exponentially with each passing year. It was always beware of this, beware of that; no one and no thing can be trusted; life is difficult and unpredictable; . . . and all those other programmed fears that continually perpetrate acts of terror on our psyches. Being constantly wary is not only limiting, but exhausting.

Fear is one of those things where less is more. Less fear leads to more joy, more happiness, more success, more abundance, and more good in all its glorious forms.

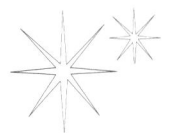
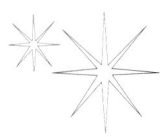

CHAPTER
11

Probably the most curious place I've seen the *Beware of Dog* sign was perched just inside the window of a small, older model RV. The turquoise-trimmed white camper with West Virginia plates was parked in the Bear Lake parking area, several miles inside Rocky Mountain National Park. I was intrigued, and I soon found myself cautiously approaching the camper, wondering whether the dangerous animal alluded to by the red and white sign might still be inside. The latched windows and darkened interior led me to believe that all of the occupants, including the dog referenced, had left at some point and not yet returned. I couldn't help but wonder why someone would choose to ride across the country in a small enclosed space with an attack pet and then decide to exercise him along a people-laden path circling a popular tourist attraction. My husband told me I was really naïve—that even if there actually *were* a dog traveling with the owners of the camper (and he seriously questioned that), he was probably more docile than dangerous. The sign, he reasoned, was akin to the fake security camera I used to have in my retail store—a calculated bluff. The *Beware of Dog* sign had no more "teeth" than my *Security Cameras on Premises* warning, he insisted.

My husband's hunch was apparently correct because less than five minutes later, an older couple, minus dog, approached the vehicle and discreetly slipped inside. Not a bark was heard. The sign was really about fear. Fear had put it there and it, in turn, used fear to keep perceived danger at a distance.

In many ways, I understood. When I had my shop, it was a constant challenge to protect my inventory from costly theft and random acts of toy abuse. Securing the entrance and exit with signs threatening the wrath of a vicious dog would not have been considered customer friendly, thus sabotaging my goal of increased sales.

The only dogs on the premises were of the plush variety, with stitched-on smiles and plastic eyes. A few did actually bark, but only with the help of two C batteries. They resided in a three-hundred-pound wooden display unit—a permanent residence we nicknamed "The Big Bad Doghouse," but the dogs were of little use in protecting even the Barbie® dolls stacked on the shelves next to them, dolls which escaped out the front door in over-sized purses, deep-pocket coats, and neoprene backpacks on a weekly basis.

Losing merchandise to shoplifting appeared to be an occupational hazard for store owners, but I never really got used to it. Every time a doll disappeared or a teddy bear went missing from its familiar location, I became more and more frustrated, retreating to my office for an Almond Joy fix—my go-to comfort candy and mood enhancer.

I'd chastise the employees for not keeping better watch; I'd reposition the overhead security mirrors and install yet another camera. There had to be a way to stop the violation. The more frightened and protective I became, the more reason I had to be so. Fear begets fear, and before I was able to remove myself from the downward spiral, I had invested more in security equipment and extra staff than I was losing by way of theft.

I wondered whether those people who post *Beware of Dog* signs weren't having some of the same undesired side effects. Putting up that two-foot-wide metal sign with bold letters, all in caps, announces to the world that you spend every day of your life in paralyzing fear, fear for your property and/or your personal well-being.

Some Beware of Dog signs, depending on their size and location, have more bite than others. For example, billboard-sized Beware of Dog signs on twelve-foot-high chain-link fences really mean business. These in-your-face signs are tantamount to someone screaming through a bullhorn, "Hey you, with the startled look on your face! Step away from the fence NOW and no one gets hurt!" Those signs definitely get my attention—I have no desire to be mauled by some ferocious canine(s) or an enraged proprietor. There was always a part of me, however, that wanted to yell back, "How dare you threaten me with some poor animal you've trained to be a one-dog combat unit!"

I am more than a little curious about who (or what) could possibly be inside those gates that so desperately needs guarding. But I am not curious enough to climb the electrified fence to find out.

Intimidating, fear-the-dog signs are actually very easy to acquire. Dozens of different versions are available for sale, some more daunting than others. *Warning, Attack Dog on Premises—No Trespassing* definitely would stop me in my tracks.

I'm sure it's no accident that these signs always seem to be supersized and posted on a massive fence-style barrier of some sort, secured by a large gate with a lock the size of a small safe. I suppose it's a matter of perspective whether the danger is being locked in or locked out. Either way, the dog is simply an unwitting pawn (albeit often a commando-trained one) in the "my-fear-is-bigger-than-your-fear" game.

With that in mind, I wonder if three-foot *Beware of Dog* signs trump two-foot ones? Are they a reflection of greater fear? The signs that have a sketch of a ferocious dog showing his large teeth right beneath the lettering definitely scream fear the loudest; I'm just not sure exactly what they are saying. "My fear is *so* big that it requires the most aggressive, confrontational sign

I can find?" And is there some fine print that, although not spelled out, is pretty much understood?

"I, the dog (real or otherwise) owner (also real or otherwise) reserve the right to post this and/or any other warning sign for one or more of the following reasons:

1. I can't control my dog, and he *may* be dangerous.
2. I've spent years training the dog to be vicious, and I *know* he is dangerous.
3. I want to scare you off. There's no dog—never has been, never will be—but I'm counting on the threat alone to keep you at bay. Basically, *I'm* dangerous.

Still, if I had to put together a "beware of" list that identified the top ten things to fear, it wouldn't include dogs. It wouldn't include animals at all. What we really need to "beware of" are the limitations we impose on ourselves because of fear.

If our fear feels the need to "beware of" something, we might want to take a lesson or three from the following tales:

Beware of anyone or anything that fences you in:
Captain, the Pit Bull

My friend lived in a quiet neighborhood that prided itself on expansive greenbelts and wide open spaces. She had a nice, roomy backyard for her dog, but the vigilant homeowner's association warned her that erecting a fence for her dog was prohibited by their covenants. Allowing Captain to run free in her yard was not an option; as obedient a dog as he was, the lure of unfenced yards and free-range squirrels would be too much of a temptation, and both she and her dog could easily find themselves on the no call (no talk to, no tolerate) list. Her solution was to install invisible electric fencing. If Captain had the urge to roam, a mild electric shock would remind him to keep his wanderlust in check.

Feeling sorry for her canine friend, who she believed must certainly had been living in fear of being shocked, she kindly removed the collar and hoped for the best. Captain was now free, or at least she thought so. Even though the warning collar had been removed, Captain went on with life as usual. He seemed completely unaware of his new owner-granted freedom. He still remained in his own yard and never strayed, convinced that moving beyond its borders would have shocking consequences.

Captain was a happy, content dog, but he had given up on pushing his boundaries long before the fence "came down." He became so bound by his comfort zone that he didn't even realize the fence that kept him there no longer even existed.

Moral: Fear the fence, especially when it only exists in the mind of the fencee.

Beware of relationships with leashes—short or otherwise: Bella, the Cairn Terrier

Grandpuppy Bella loves to go for walks. If you move within ten feet of the closet containing her leash, she begins her crazy going-for-a-walk dance, wildly jumping up and down while swinging her head from side to side and flapping her tongue back and forth, spraying spit three feet in every direction. Even though she knows the leash restricts her rabbit chasing to twelve feet per pursuit, she's willing to work within that limitation in order to strut her stuff as queen of the block for at least a little while.

Her leash is a *Princess Peak*, adorned with beaucoup bling, and has an extra long extension, a flash light for night strolls, and a AM/FM radio that plays her fave tunes, but it's still a leash, and Bella's subject to Grandpa's timetable, his temperamental gout foot, and whether or not he remembered to bring his heavy coat.

Anything that restricts your ability to express yourself openly and freely, as only you can, even if it sparkles and has all the bells, whistles, and sexy upgrades you've always dreamed of, is still a leash.

Moral: A leash by any other name is still a leash, and you aren't going anywhere as long as you agree to be tethered.

Beware of fear coming back to bite you:
Macintosh, the Carlin Pinscher

Little Macintosh is a ball of black fur with the energy of a hyper roadrunner. For a small dog, he can create enough commotion to exasperate ten to twelve adults at a time. But Mac is irresistible. He'll snuggle in the crick of your arm and stare lovingly into your eyes . . . most of the time. Occasionally, without any warning, he'll leap up and bite your nose, and then settle back into his cuddle place for a short snooze. You can't predict when he's going to do it, but you know it's always a possibility. I think that's the way he likes it. He can smell your fear. When it's at its peak, when you've checked five times in thirty seconds to make sure he's not in attack-ready stance, he knows it's time to act. It's a three-step process. Jump up. Chomp! Go limp and pretend to sleep. It's a wicked mind game: dog vs. gullible dog lover, but he's *so* adorable. I'm pretty sure he wouldn't bite people if they bit him back, if they stood up to him—all twenty one inches of him.

Moral: Life may catch us by surprise, but being a victim is always optional.

What really threatens us is allowing fear to rule our lives, giving our power to others, turning our backs on our unlimited potential, and failing to feed our spirits. Unfortunately, there are no rectangular metal signs with red block lettering to warn us against any of these things.

Rather than create more signs telling us what to fear, maybe we should create ones that help us learn what to embrace. We're doing just that, of course, when we use affirmations— when we post sticky notes all over our bathroom mirrors with encouraging messages, such as, "I choose Love," "I am the peace I wish to experience," "I trust my whole life to spirit," "I will start my diet on Monday," and so forth. These might look a little odd posted on someone's front gate, but they'd sure attract attention.

After ten years of shots, I've resolved my allergy issues with dogs (and other animals), and gotten over my canine commitment phobia. As soon as my kids left home, the first thing they all did was get a dog or two. I'm now a victim of puppy love thanks to Bella, Kobe, Maddie, and Mac—who always greet me enthusiastically with wet dog kisses, whether it's been a week or a year since we were last together. I absolutely cherish my time with these loving and lov*able* pets. They are just as eager to see me on bad hair days as on good ones, they are always ready to play at the drop of a ball, they encourage me to take nice long walks to stay healthy, they never let me stray too far, they snuggle with me when my heart is hurting, and they never miss a chance to let me know that I am loved and appreciated. What I most cherish about these beloved dogs, though, is that they remind me of who I really am. Their dark eyes pierce deep into my soul, reaching out to that divine being within me who occasionally gets a little lost.

Beware of what you are wary of. We give our fear bite when we turn it against others, which, in turn, turns it against us. Contrary to what we may believe, it's our own *fear* that bites us in the butt. It nips at our heels, it snaps at us, its bark keeps us up all night, it jumps on us and tackles us, it sniffs our breath to see if we're still alive, and then it bites again.

I wonder whether anyone ever made a "Beware of Fear" sign. I'd buy it.

Please Do Not Open Packages

I tear into my birthday gift like I'm expecting to find a Rolls-Royce® in a beribboned package not much bigger than a breadbox. It's possible, I tell myself, that the small box was simply meant to throw me off. Cleverly hidden inside are the keys to my dream ride, and the actual car is parked down the block with a bow the size of a Great Dane affixed to its roof. When I realize the package actually contains a pair of bunny slippers that look like mutant hamsters, I'm not amused. I'm not just let down—I'm angry. I had a forty-two-item wish list posted on the refrigerator for three months and bedroom slippers (of any kind) weren't even one of the options! Why didn't I get what I wanted? Why are all my surprises disappointments? What am I going to do with scuffs that look like dead rodents?

We may not always get what we ask for, but we do always get what we're open to receive. Expecting disappointment all but guarantees that's exactly what we'll get. It's tantamount to releasing a prayer into the universe requesting the perfect manifestation of our worst-case scenario. Expectations can be landmines along our spiritual path, making it virtually impossible to get to the good that God intends for us. Life is filled with gifts, many of which go unnoticed and unopened. Others are opened, but quickly discarded because we're unable to see their value.

When gifts don't meet the expectations we've outlined, we often don't even recognize the opened packages as gifts at all. Those slippers will keep me warmer than flannel PJ's during a mid-winter cold snap, and my wood floors will never need dusting again.

Here are my gift-receiving guidelines:

- The real fun is in discovering the gift, no matter what's inside the package.
- The gift, regardless of its size or nature, just gives. Receiving it—that's entirely optional.
- The secret to having everything I want is to feel gratitude for everything I receive.

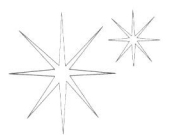
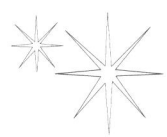

CHAPTER
12

I've been told I enjoyed opening gifts when I was a little girl. My mom had the hard evidence (i.e., photos) to prove it. There I was at age five, sitting cross-legged in front of our ho-ho-ho, traditional, tinsel-trimmed Christmas tree with a wide, toothy smile, lovingly snuggling my new Toni doll with the perfectly permed hair. And there I was again at six, seven, eight (etc.) posed in front of a clone of the previous year's Yule spruce, with my signature holiday grin, proudly displaying some representative sample of Santa's generosity.

Birthday photos were little more than a variation on the same theme. There was no spruced-up spruce backdrop for these Kodak memories; instead, I was posed in front of an artfully arranged balloon bouquet that was anchored to the back leg of our overstuffed sofa. There I was at my fifth, sixth, seventh, and eighth (etc.) birthday parties, seated on the familiar couch surrounded by an updated group of BFFs, grinning gleefully behind a large stack of gaily wrapped gifts piled on my lap. Yes, there was proof—in fact, an entire shoebox full—but I wasn't buying what the girl in the photos was selling.

Maybe it was after the cruel substitution of a forgettable Miss Nobody fashion doll for the A-list Little Miss Revlon I'd been dreaming about; maybe it was after I was given accordion lessons, even though I'd made it absolutely clear that my heart's desire was to play an instrument that didn't belch air and was destined for something greater than polka music; or maybe it was the realization that I wasn't going to get Sleeping Beauty's chiffon-draped canopy bed with bluebirds circling its posts in a room I could call my own. Whatever the cause, by age nine, I'd lost interest in opening gifts. I loved yards of multi-colored curling ribbon and festive papers as much as the next kid, but once I tore through the elaborately camouflaged packages, were the contents going to live up to the hype? A nine-year-old skeptic is a sad thing.

How had I become so cynical at such a young age? Were my well-meaning but clueless parents at fault? Was our struggling-to-get-by lifestyle to blame? Or perhaps distrust had been somehow imbedded in my genetic code? Surely, there had to be some root cause for my misery.

After careful consideration, I decided that the source of my cynicism was Marshall Field's. A grand, multi-level department store in downtown Chicago, Marshall Field's was my first exposure to retail nirvana. My second exposure was the next best thing to actually being there: the Marshall Field's Christmas Toy Catalogue. Within the pages of that mesmerizing publication lived elegantly costumed dolls, mega-marvelous toys, and fantastical plush creatures beyond anything I could have ever dreamed up on my own. And reveling in this glorious bounty of wondrous gifts were glowingly happy, smiling children, apparently having their every wish granted with one flourish of Marshall's magic wand. Marshall Field's was the cosmic treasure chest overflowing with wishes fulfilled.

It wasn't *that* crazy an idea. I'd been to the actual Marshall Field's store in downtown Chicago during the holidays, and it was Santa's Workshop, Cinderella's Castle, and Oompa Loompa Land all rolled into one. I'd had lunch in view of the heart-stopping multi-story Christmas tree with colossal, fantasy packages beneath its boughs. I'd crossed the threshold of Toy Land and seen the King Kong-sized teddy bears and batteries-not-included wonder toys. I'd even seen the snow-globe-like animated holiday scenes that came to life daily in the State Street windows, complete with softly falling snowflakes and animated singing dolls. And I'd even sat in Santa's lap at the Cozy Cloud Cottage and been assured that my Christmas would be everything Marshall Field's and I could imagine together. I knew this place was enchanted.

I wanted what those catalogue kids were having. I was quite sure from their smug, not-a-care-in-the-world expressions that they all had at least one of everything shown in the Christmas book. In addition, I strongly suspected—even though I might never be able to prove it—that these children also had fabulously rich parents, relied on hired servants to do their chores, never suffered through childhood illnesses, and never *ever* had to share *anything* with their siblings.

In my world, on the other hand, parents scraped to get by, kids were forced to make their own beds, and contagious diseases were passed down from one child to another like outgrown tennis shoes. I waited, year after year, for the Marshall Field's truck to show up at my door and deliver me from my sad lot.

I once kept an unopened Christmas gift hidden under my bed for two years. It was from my grandmother, and I was fairly certain it contained a couple of plain white undershirts with scratchy lace trim. What I'd asked for was the giant five-foot-tall, super-soft, caramel-colored teddy bear with a "festive red velvet bow" I'd seen in—where else—the Marshall Field's toy catalogue. It was apparent by the fifteen-inch square, one-inch deep package that, regardless of how much I wanted it to be otherwise (remember, these were the days before Build-A-Bear stores), there wasn't a sixty-inch teddy bear with a fetching stitched-on grin concealed inside.

When my mother finally discovered the box during one of her annual spring cleaning fervors, she insisted that I open it and apologize to my grandmother. I said my "I'm sorry" over and over and was forgiven. By the way, it did, indeed, contain two white undershirts, which were now way too small. That was fine with me.

It was in the fall of that same year that I found out the "Santa's helper," who dropped by our apartment with a bounty of gifts every Christmas Eve, was actually my parents' friend, Kenny, dressed in a red fuzzy costume with a sadly obvious fake beard. It was the same holiday season I discovered that the gargantuan packages beneath the towering Marshall Field's tree were actually empty boxes decorated to *look* like fabulous Christmas gifts. I'd clearly been betrayed or, at the very least, "bah-humbugged." Where was my miracle on State Street? I was in desperate need of someone to rescue me from the realities of the cold, hopelessly cruel world (and from my passion for drama). It was easy to spiral down into an eggnog cup-half-empty perspective on life, and I took comfort in feeling sorry for myself.

What was the point of becoming aware of all the fabulous things the world had to offer if they were either built on illusion or not available to me anyway?

Forty years and three kids of my own later, not a whole lot had changed. In my adult world, the Marshall Field's catalogue had been replaced by home shopping clubs and late night infomercials. My longing for a 1:4 scale dollhouse, a lady doll with an eighty-two piece wardrobe, and room-size, super-soft stuffed animals was replaced, instead, by industrial grade food choppers that could slice and dice whole pineapples in four seconds, carving knives fit for a samurai, and face creams that transformed you from an ugly stepsister to Angelina Jolie (and if you ordered within the next twenty minutes, Brad Pitt was thrown in as a bonus).

As an adult, I didn't have to rely on my parents to buy me the things that were my heart's desire in the television catalogue, and I didn't have to wait until Christmas; Visa had a better inventory than Santa anyway and our friendly local UPS driver was one of their many helpers. But, even when I had control over the contents of the pretty packages I received (I always ordered the optional gift-wrapping even if I was buying it for myself), it didn't really work out any better.

I once decided to surprise myself with the gift of diamond heart earrings that I found for the "unbelievably affordable blowout price of only $24.95" on a popular shopping channel. No more CZs for me, I thought! The image of the earrings, nestled in the velvet lined gift box, filled the entire screen of my fifty-two-inch TV, and the sparkle from the precious stones sent me running for my shades. After I placed my order for these "show stopper" earrings, I began to worry that I might need extra large backings to support their weight. When they arrived, I realized that I had fretted needlessly. Rather than being large enough to cause lobe damage, they were more appropriately sized for Barbie.

Expectations can leave even the most Pollyanna personalities among us deeply disappointed. I *deserved* a pair of big, bold, bodacious diamond earrings; there was precious little bling in my life, and I was bitter. Even Visa couldn't help me out—there were limits to how much happiness it would allow me to buy for myself, and I had spent most of my life butting up against and/or exceeding those limits, but I still didn't have what I wanted.

My real issue wasn't a destined-to-be-disappointed life or a lackluster financial portfolio, but rather some misplaced expectations I'd been harboring since childhood.

Many of us have saddled ourselves with a couple of sorely misguided beliefs: (1) We deserve more than we have—no matter what we already have, we still deserve *more* because, apparently, there's *more* out there to be had and we wouldn't want to miss out, and (2) It's up to the universe (via Mom, Dad, Santa, Easter Bunny, Wall Street, ZapposShoes.com, etc.) to provide it for us. As children, our expectations may be focused on more of the newest dolls/toys/video game systems; as adults, we expect more by way of a six-figure dream job, a fourteen-day cruise to Hawaii, a bestselling book which leads to an Oprah Winfrey Network appearance, and blissful relationships that thrive in spite of our clueless attempts to destroy them. We expect that our bodies won't age if we keep getting enough facelifts, and that the old saying, "You're not getting older, you're getting better," means our mature years will be defined by diamonds and not Depends®. We're always expecting, but the universe never seems to get around to delivering our little bundle of "joy."

Every "package" we open, whether it's a special delivery box from QVC, a letter from a prospective employer, or an- e-mail response to a book query is a letdown waiting to happen if we don't understand that *every* package is a gift, regardless of its contents. Learning to expect the gift, rather than the disappointment, can make opening packages a pleasant and even inspiring experience.

I have a friend who finds nothing more inviting than a taped box, wrapped gift, or sealed package. Insatiable curiosity kicks in, and she can't wait to see what's hidden inside. Ripping off glistening bows and tearing through decorative wrap is a cherished ritual of possibility that she approaches with bountiful enthusiasm. Even when the newly exposed box has pictures on the outside clearly showing its contents, it doesn't slow her down a bit; she still can't resist. Sure, she knows from the illustration on the side of the carton that it's the punch bowl she was gushing over at the home goods store, but the thought of actually holding it in her hands and examining every facet of the gold-colored iridescent cut glass is almost too much for her to bear. She voraciously tears through the heavy staples and tan industrial tape to reveal the contents. The process is both amusing and heartwarming to watch. Her joy in discovery is infectious, and you find yourself wishing you'd bought her one for every room in the house. How could anyone be that deliriously happy about a large glass bowl with a plastic ladle and twelve matching cups?

Then again, she gets that excited about every gift she receives. She believes that every package she opens contains something fabulous, the absolutely ideal thing meant just for her.

Her unwavering faith in the perfection of life was inspiring, even if it was a little puzzling at times.

My husband lost his father at a young age and spent most of his pre-adult years in a place called "Child City," operated by the Loyal Order of Moose. Although the children who lived there were well cared-for, it was still essentially an orphanage and the kids rarely received presents, which meant they had very little to call their own. At Christmas, they were given a short list of possible gifts (absolutely none of which came out of any eye-popping toy catalogue) and were allowed to check their top three choices. Getting one of those choices made for a happy holiday; getting a second or even a third gift was a Christmas fantasy come true.

Bob remembers one year in particular when, in addition to their allotted presents, the boys were given special gifts made just for them by a local group of "Mrs. Santas." He recalls the boys' surprise when more than a hundred pairs of handmade boxer shorts showed up in festively wrapped packages. Undeterred by the somewhat underwhelming gift, the grand opening was followed by an impromptu parade of boxer-clad teen boys prancing through every room of the dorm singing "Jingle Bells." In one evening, the guys shattered the age-old myth that getting underwear for Christmas is a disappointment.

A gift, regardless of its size or nature, can do nothing less than give. Whether or not we receive the gift (with appreciation) is entirely optional. There is no gift that doesn't have value. Those seemingly lackluster undershirts from my grandmother had handsewn lace along the neckline and sleeves, and a tiny bow from Grandma Marge's cache of satin ribbons. Tucked in with those shirts was the priceless gift of love and time.

When our gifts don't show up in quite the way we outline, we often don't even recognize them. The secret to having everything we want is in being able to see the potential in everything we receive.

My grandson's second Christmas was a particularly bountiful event for the little eighteen-month-old. Presents wrapped in cartoon character-themed paper and bearing his name were piled so high, they blocked out the light from the living room windows. Winnie-the-Pooh packages were stacked on Spiderman packages which were stacked on Sponge Bob packages which were stacked on . . . well, you get the idea.

At the appointed hour, only minutes after finishing off the last spoonfuls of our family's traditional "Heavenly Hash" holiday dessert, everyone adjourned to the living room for the Christmas Eve package opening ritual. Uncle Derek distributed the presents, placing little Aidan's in a row of stair-step-style stacks in front of him. The toddler studied them for a couple of minutes, flashed a full-face smile, and began to climb up on the gifts, gingerly crawling back and forth from one pile to the next, totally wrapped up in the joy his gifts were providing. Although his parents eventually were able to coax him down off the impromptu jungle gym with promises of frosting-laden "cake-cake" and got him to concentrate on actually opening the packages, it was clear that he enjoyed them wrapped and stacked at least as much as he did unwrapped and spread out in front of him. He was too young to have made a Christmas list or to understand expectations and disappointments, but he was wise beyond his year and a half in his ability to enjoy what he found outside the box as well as inside. Those packages brought him joy in more than just the jingle bell holiday way.

Although I didn't realize it at the time, that Christmas catalogue of my youth actually limited my ability to see the universe of infinite possibilities that lay just beyond its few dozen glossy pages of holiday-season-only gifts. And the empty packages beneath the Marshall Field's Christmas tree weren't empty at all—they were filled with the hopes and dreams of everyone who, like me, fantasized about their contents.

The big empty boxes under the Marshall Field's Christmas tree of my childhood gave the gift of wonder, their larger-than-life size sparking the imagination of every child and adult that passed by. Each box contained exactly what the observer believed it did. Anything *but* empty, those packages held the fantasies of thousands tucked neatly beneath their lids.

Those fantastical packages were stuffed with sugar plum visions of everything from giggling Muppet dolls, to Trump-worthy mansions. They undoubtedly also housed less tangible dreams, like finding that perfect life partner or pursuing a fulfilling career.

We've come to believe that packages wrapped in pretty papers and adorned with starchy bows are an unspoken promise of wonderful things to come. When we pop the lid of our so-called gift and what we find inside isn't what we hoped for, we blame the package, we blame the giver, we blame the circumstances, and we blame God. But perhaps the blame lies within us.

What would happen if we reexamined the "package" contents from a greater perspective? It is possible that those gifts which appear, at first, to be disappointing can open the door to greater joy than the gift we *thought* we wanted could ever provide. The gifts of imagination, of learning, of growing, of loving, of understanding, of compassion . . . and the list goes on . . . long outlast the perceived value of anything we might have checked off on a pen-and-paper list.

Did I actually have to receive every one of the toys in the Christmas book to be able to experience their gift? As I paged through the catalogue, the one I looked forward to for months, enjoying its wondrous offerings, I could imagine myself tickling each fluffy teddy bear, getting hopefully lost in the pages of each storybook, and sharing Eskimo kisses with each baby doll. The real gift had already been given, and it had very little to do with whether or not the toys I thought I wanted showed up in packages tucked beneath our Christmas tree. Joy is the greatest gift we can receive and that joy was in the catalogue itself.

It was the same gift I was given every time I oohed and aahed over the magnificent packages beneath the Marshall Field's Christmas tree. Just imagining what was in those big boxes provided more joy than the perceived contents ever could have.

At nine years old, I wasn't ready to hear or understand the message that it is not the gift that disappoints us, it's our limited ability to see its value. Nobody or nothing had denied me anything; in fact, there was an ever-increasing stack of gifts piling up in front of me. I just couldn't see them.

Not finding what I want inside a lavishly wrapped gift package is more about me than it is about the package contents. No disrespect to magic wands intended, but nothing inside that package or any other is ever going to transform me from the poor Cinderella of my perception into the deliriously happy, flawlessly beautiful, handsome-Prince-magnet Cinderella of my dreams—the one who rode off into the sunset with her soul-mate, a fairy godmother, and a lifetime guarantee that her every wish would be granted.

I can open packages for the rest of my life and never find the gift that can do that for me. Sometimes old adages really do bear repeating: "Happiness is an inside job" is one of them. It reminds me that finding value in what's inside a gift package is entirely up to us. *We* may even be the package ourselves, but we rarely turn inward long enough to make that discovery. Instead, we open package after package after package, looking for the one that will give us what we fear *isn't* within us: the experience of true happiness. There is nothing inside a box and outside of me that can ever provide that. That's why some of the greatest gifts we receive don't come in packages at all.

How could you box up the gift of love? There wouldn't be a container big enough to hold it. How could you package the gift of self-esteem or self-acceptance? Even if you could, no one could ever give you that gift except yourself. The gift of spiritual awareness is divinely given and is rarely ever even fully unwrapped in our current lifetime. The best part is that these gifts always live up to and far exceed our expectations.

Even the more traditional gifts can never disappoint us if we look for the value we receive from them. Sometimes we don't even have to unwrap a package to find the gift it bears. That small box of chocolate cherries your five-year-old tucks into a sandwich bag and decorates with a crayon drawing of a heart tucked just beneath a stick-on bow carries a value of "priceless." Finding a way to celebrate the gifts we receive puts the fun back into unwrapping presents. Looking for the real value in everything that shows up in our lives transforms every moment into a joy-filled experience.

Our willingness to keep opening every gift we're presented with, and blessing the contents, keeps the gifts coming. Each gift opened, each chance taken, each shift made, invites greater and greater gifts into our lives.

Please do not open packages unless you are prepared to be awed and amazed.

Please do not open packages unless you are ready to receive unconditionally.

Please do not open packages unless you can open your heart to the infinite gifts the universe has to offer . . . and be joyful.

Free To Good Home

Sure, I've heard it said that "the best things in life are free" and I almost believe it. Yes, the view of the Colorado mountains is breathtaking; hugs from friends are the feel-good moments of my day; and the puppy paw prints on my new white leather couch remind me of the value of forgiveness.

But when it comes to spiritual growth, I keep looking for the price tag. I'm absolutely convinced that unless I attend a minimum of two retreats a year, purchase a monthly subscription to Spiritual Cinema Circle, or read at least one Deepak Chopra book a week, I'll never find enlightenment!

I've followed my favorite guru to Tibet in winter, Mexico in summer, and Kansas during April-June; I've just added a sixth bookshelf to my den to handle the comprehensive library of spiritual self-help titles, and I've added a second altar to my meditation room to accommodate my growing collection of Om candles. Yet, I'm as lost and confused as ever.

The truth is, spiritual evolution is always FREE to a "good home"—a consciousness of love, joy, acceptance, compassion, and peace. No book/class/movie/workshop/retreat can fulfill me with that which is already within. Those outside resources may help keep me motivated, but they are no substitute for consciously co-creating a good home from within. So, I trade in my frequent flyer miles for some quiet, at-home time with spirit. Once I get my spiritual house in order, my good home will attract the best of everything.

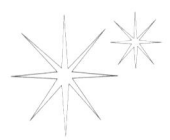
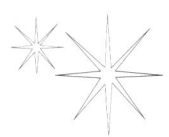

CHAPTER
13

My oldest daughter always liked bunnies. Even though her aunt painted two large, eye-popping Raggedy Ann and Andy figures on the bedroom wall, and I populated her shelves with grinning yarn-haired dolls in a variety of sizes, she never really bonded with the button-eyed bunch. She preferred to hang out in her little sister's Peter Rabbit-themed nursery. Even though she was barely three years old, it was clear she coveted her sister's rabbit room.

Every morning after naptime, she would snatch a few of her Raggedy clan from one of the lower shelves, drag them by one leg, heads bouncing off the floor leaving a telltale trail of yarn-fuzz breadcrumbs all the way to her sister's room, and unceremoniously dump them in her sister's crib. Then she would exchange them for as many plush bunnies as she could carry (and/or stuff under her shirt) back to her bedroom.

I figured it was some kind of furry friends phase and, since allergy issues prevented us from having live pets in the house, I didn't make too big a deal of the ritualistic exchange of playthings each morning. As she grew older, the seemingly benign cuddly bunny phase evolved into a full-blown Phase Two—"The Obsession." She began coveting everything bunny-related. Rows of stuffed rabbits lined the walls of her bedroom, dozens more hung from the ceiling in "pet nets," and her bed became home to several plush bunny families, who took up permanent residence with their ever-expanding brood atop her Peter Rabbit quilt. Every time I opened the door to her room, there seemed to be more occupants, somehow magically multiplying overnight while I slept, blissfully unaware of the population explosion going on in the room next to mine.

Soon porcelain rabbit figurines of all shapes and sizes began appearing on her shelves, bunny slippers were parked permanently under her bed, and rabbit-themed jackets, sweatshirts, undies, knee-highs, and nightgowns packed her bulging closet. The Monday after Easter (when everything bunny went on sale for half price at local stores) became a high holy day and standing in line at Target waiting for the doors to open was a sacred ritual to be observed in silence, sipping black coffee from the convenience store across the street.

It was the day after a particularly frenzied Easter clearance sale one year that I finally raised the white "Garden Bunnies" outdoor flag in surrender. Allergies be damned. I threw caution to the wind, stocked up on antihistamines, and agreed to the addition of a pet rabbit to the family . . . *when* the time was right.

The right time came sooner than expected. Crystal was an accidental, or as Dawn would have characterized it, "pre-destined, synchronistic" garage sale find. I was on the hunt for a small desk that would fit in the corner of the kitchen, and this particular sale advertised "tons of furniture." It was only a few blocks from our house, so I decided to swing by on the way to the grocery store. The sale lived up to its ad, with dressers, tables, and dining chairs strewn all over the front lawn. However, my quick visual inventory failed to locate even one desk, and I considered moving on.

Then I saw her. Off to the side of the driveway, just beneath an aspiring young Russian Olive tree, was a handmade wooden hutch with a spotted brown Mini Lop cuddled in the corner.

A yellow cardboard sign with a handwritten message in blue marker that read, "Free to Good Home" was attached to the front of the cage with a couple yards of masking tape.

I remember thinking how interesting it was that the owner was asking twenty-five dollars for a glass-top coffee table with a canyon-deep crack running halfway down the center, but was offering the big-eyed pet bunny free of charge.

I approached the cage and was leaning down to get a better look, when, alas, "Crystal" began speaking to me "telepathically" through a series of puffy little thought bubbles (like the ones they have in comic strips) that floated just above her head.

It may have been a rare hallucinatory side-effect of downing three cups of coffee in less than thirty minutes earlier that morning, but what follows is a word-for-word transcript of the very personal (and clearly embellished for dramatic effect in order to play on my sympathies) saga of love and loss I "heard" that day.

Alas, I began my life journey as a humble Easter bunny, cruelly separated from my mother and siblings shortly after my birth by bunny brokers who shoved me in a dreary, dark box and shipped me off to an undersized and over-decorated mall pet emporium.

There I was put on display in a bare-bones wire cage adorned with an oversized, green-glittered bow tied to one of the top bars, marketed as a holiday gift, and sold with a "basket bonus" containing a half dozen neon pink plastic eggs and a couple of crudely formed, foil-wrapped chocolate chicks.

At first the children were delighted with their Easter gift and fought over who would attend to my daily care. I was hugged, petted, and showered with loving words. They spoke to me in some kind of odd language that included purring sounds similar to those I've heard emanating from cats, but this version was gushing with affection.

I was watered and fed until I feared I was going to pop. My daily all-you-can-eat buffet of leafy lettuce and crunchy carrots was turning my whiskers a fetching shade of green and my fur was beginning to flash shiny orange highlights. I was blissfully happy. Then slowly over time, my "good home" became a house of horrors. I was banished to a hutch in the garage, had only occasional human contact, and was fed dry pellets once a day. When I was carried out (hutch and all) to the front yard for this garage sale, it was the first time in weeks I'd felt the warmth of the sun on my floppy ears, and my heart hopped with hope. Maybe the good home of my dreams was going to become a reality after all. And then with one final sigh, she whispered, *"Are you my new Mommy?"*

Having noticed me hanging out by the bunny hutch, the owner rushed over to greet me before I had a chance to turn my attention elsewhere. At first she gushed about the cute little rabbit (now staring at me with pleading, hopeful eyes), but eventually confessed that, although the bunny had started out as the family's "Cuddlemuffin," the required daily attention, conscious care, and five-pound bag of custom-blended rabbit food she ate every month had become a burden. (Ah ha! So Crystal *was* telling the truth . . .) As if to answer my mental aside, the woman also shared that the bunny was cared for and loved as best they could manage while they searched for a new home, spending her days in the well-lighted, heated, converted garage they used for a family room. (Ok, so Crystal was exaggerating a *little*).

Crystal had just become too high maintenance. She required more money, time, and attention than this family was able (or willing) to provide.

Yet, they still wanted a happily ever after for their pet rabbit. So although Crystal was offered for "free," there was some "fine print"—conditions that needed to be met before she would be handed over. The requirement was this: whoever adopted

Crystal would have to agree to provide her with a good home. They weren't expecting her new family to supply a personal groomer, a live-in chef, and a split-level hutch with a sunroom; a good home simply meant one where time, attention, loving care, and a life-sustaining supply of rabbit food were readily available. It didn't seem like all that much to ask in exchange for a furry little puff of unconditional love.

Just because something is free doesn't mean it's without value. Crystal had lots of value, and most of it was of the intangible kind: love, affection, companionship, and *endless entertainment*. For example, did you know that bunny's mouths turn lipstick red after eating strawberries? And like lipstick, that color can be transferred to anyone or anything, adding a whole new dimension to the "lipstick on your collar" dilemma? Yes, Crystal was a valuable addition to our family. When something has value for us, it makes sense that it should be handled with loving care. Taking care of something is giving it a good home.

If we can figure out how to provide a good home for a pet, surely we can come up with some strategies for providing a good home for ourselves. We can begin by cleaning up our consciousness so we can actually enjoy "living" there. The same principles apply.

We have all built a spiritual house of some kind, whether we realize it or not. What we believe and don't believe, how we behave and don't behave, what we value and don't value, all impact exactly what that house looks like and how comfortable it feels. Our spiritual home—whether it's a classic two-story, sprawling ranch style, tri-level, mountain cabin with outdoor plumbing, etc.—however it may look, belongs to us. We've built it with our thoughts, actions, and re-actions.

I must admit that at times, mine has looked a lot like a fun house. Not the kind where life is a constant joy ride and merriment abounds, unfortunately, but more like the kind of fun house you find at amusement parks. These "the joke's on you" brand of fun houses have mirrors that reflect back to you your worst nightmare, a maze of corridors going nowhere that trap you inside its dark interior, and narrow passages lined with rotating barrels that constantly throw you off balance.

As a kid, I willingly handed over my babysitting money to spend time in those crazy houses where floors didn't stay put under my feet, my senses deceived me, and even gravity was not completely reliable. There was a little rush of excitement in the unpredictability of it all. Yet even then, I knew it didn't make sense to set up permanent residence there.

Most of us are pretty *un*conscious when it comes to providing a good spiritual home for our consciousness. We do it by trial and error, kind of haphazardly, with no regard for basic building principles, such as starting with a solid foundation, using only quality materials, making sure everything is up to God-code, and checking to see that the house is built according to a well-drafted design plan. Instead, we build our spiritual home through trial and error, from a plan drawn on an Etch-A-Sketch®

out of whatever's available at the time, with minimal regard for livability or long-term investment potential. As long as it looks pretty good on the surface, we convince ourselves that we've created a good home, even if it's really all smoke and mirrors with a little outright deception thrown into the mix.

When my sister Myrna was in grammar school, she and my mother struggled daily over the condition of her room. To call it chaos was to do that word a disservice. It was far worse than that and even worse still. It looked as though someone had stood in the doorway and tossed clothing, books, dolls, games, sports balls, and a few random pieces of Melmac into the space as part of some carnival midway game gone wrong. There were no prizes won for the condition of this room, but my brothers did seem to enjoy watching my mother morph into a screaming banshee every time she opened the door and viewed the devastation left behind by tornado Myrna. Mom tried every approach possible to get my sister to tidy her room. "A messy room means a messy mind," she would say, and learning to consciously maintain order in her life would have lasting benefits well beyond just a pretty place to sleep. Myrna was ok with a messy mind, so anything Mom said beyond that became "bla bla bla bla bla."

I'm not sure what the threat was that seemed to turn things around (loss of television privileges, general grounding, or mandatory attendance at family meals), but one Monday morning everything changed. The once disorderly bedroom was now the picture of *Better Homes and Gardens* perfection. The floor was cleared of treasures and trash, the bed was neatly made, and even the dresser was free of homeless plush pets.

Mom was elated, showering my sister with complements, hugs, and freshly baked Snickerdoodles. For the following week, every day after she left for school, Mom would peak into her room and, sure enough, it remained as neat and tidy as the morning before, and Mom was beside herself with joy.

It may have been my sister's apparent obsession with wearing the same blue striped sweater and black slacks to school each day, or the bed sheets that somehow remained clothesline fresh even after a full week of use, or, perhaps, the subtle trail of cookie crumbs that lead from the doorway to the bed and then disappeared beneath the dust ruffle where the fabric met the headboard, but my mother began to suspect that something was amiss.

I knew she was doing a little detective work when I found her poking around in my sister's room while she was away—learning how to darn socks at her Brownies meeting. Then later that night, I spied her checking on Myrna as she slept.

The next morning, my mother confronted my sister with the results of her investigation. From the steam emitting from her ears, I suspected it was going to be a long time before Myrna was going to see the light of day and even longer before homemade cookies made with love would find their way into her lunchbox.

Apparently, Mom's afternoon investigation had revealed a dark, hidden world of clothing, books, dolls, toys, sports balls, and plastic plates (with cookie crumb residue), shoved under the bed, nicely camouflaged by the slightly-too-long bed skirt. To make things worse, her midnight sleuthing had revealed something even more sinister—my sister, sleeping fully clothed (in her blue striped sweater and black slacks, which she had worn for five straight days) on top of her neatly made bed.

Myrna got away with it for a little while, but it was inevitable that her hastily formulated plan would eventually be exposed. Soon, she'd run out of space under the bed, and stuff would begin oozing out into the room, encroaching on the open space. And even though the bed sheets might remain crisp and clean, the passion pink posies on the "Spring Garden" bedspread would begin to wither and wilt over time, and the scent of unlaundered clothing would eventually reach out and gag someone.

Alas, on the surface, Myrna's bedroom seemed like a sweet-dreams home, but it was crumbling beneath her even as she slept.

Regardless of how over-scheduled and under-planned our lives are, there are no shortcuts to creating a good spiritual home and, no, we can't buy one on eBay. If the one we currently live in is more a house of horrors than a happy home, we may need to move out (of denial) and start over from the ground up. Continuing to add on to a structure with a shaky foundation is like constructing a house on a fault line . . . in an *active* fault zone.

It's also a lot like the leaning towers of boxes in my basement. I begin with a modest-sized file box filled with books or magazines that I'm setting aside until I have time to read them (aka permanent storage), which I shove up against a wall. A few weeks later, I add a similar-sized box containing miscellaneous glassware from my annual clean sweep of the kitchen cabinets, which I will sort through when I find a few extra minutes (aka more permanent storage).

A couple months later, I decide to add a larger box filled with cancelled checks from 1997 that I'm transferring from the upstairs closet to the basement because I haven't yet had time to shred them (see storage classification above).

It would make more sense to put this bigger box on the bottom, but I'm in a hurry and don't want to bother, so I just rest it on top. As time goes by, the stack of "I'll take care of it when I have time" boxes continues to grow, and bigger and bigger boxes seem to end up on top, all supported by that original, but now slightly crushed, small box of books and magazines at the bottom. Although I created the increasingly precarious leaning tower myself, I'm somehow startled when I hear crashing noises coming from the basement in the middle of Sunday brunch. If I'd taken the time to rebuild my pile each time I added something, making sure to place the largest, sturdiest box on the bottom and arranging the upper ones according to some sort of overall PLAN, in a balanced pile, I wouldn't be picking up pieces of broken bud vases, and gathering scattered receipts off the basement floor. Although I understand that piling up storage boxes in random order with big ones on top of small ones, on top of big ones, on top of broken-down ones, is eventually going to topple my tower, I don't take the time to strengthen my foundation and re-stack the boxes from the ground up. To make things worse, much of my tower is being built with boxes of *unfinished business* and needless clutter, making it awkwardly larger than necessary.

Regular de-cluttering and prompt updating / remodeling help maintain a good spiritual home. Having the wisdom to know when the foundation has been irreparably compromised and when it's time to call in the wrecking crew is invaluable.

It saves a lot of time and aggravation if we can catch founda-tion damage early and better still, if we can prevent it entirely. How do we do that? It starts with forgiveness. Nothing puts cracks in our foundation (or deepens the ones that are already there) faster than resentment. Resentment is a choice, which makes it preventable. It takes wisdom to know that resentment compromises one's foundation. An unwillingness to forgive has been the undoing of many spiritual homes, even those with lots of promise and a semi-load of good intentions. No good thing has ever come from holding a grudge, hanging on to anger, or wallowing in righteous indignation. One of my favorite quotes (and I have no idea who said it) is, "Resentment is like taking poison and expecting the other person to die." It's also like tak-ing a jackhammer to your own foundation and expecting the house next door to fall down.

Once we've moved beyond resentment, we can build a foun-dation of love, compassion, and joy. And once we've created a strong spiritual foundation, we can start building and/or rebuilding the rest of the house.

Abundance, health, relationships, and right employment are rooms in everyone's spiritual house, regardless of design. We're all unique and so are our spiritual homes. Whether your consciousness has constructed a two-story with a main floor master, a split-level with a spacious family room, or a rambling ranch with an unfinished basement, for example, if your life experiences in any of the rooms in your house have been less than divine, it may be time to call in an interior designer. (That's **you** co-creating with spirit.) It's your home and in this case, the work that needs to be done can't be hired out. Here are a few suggestions to help begin the process.

Abundance

An abundance of what? Abundance simply means a lot of . . . something. What do we want an abundance *of*? We want it all. And we've grown to believe that the most efficient way to have it all is through manifesting lots and lots of money. But abundance is about more than just cash and when you have an abundance of all good things in your life, money is only a small part of a much larger picture. So, here's how it works.

Rejoicing in the gifts of the universe provides a good home for abundance to thrive and prosper. Whether it's an abundance of money in our bank account, an abundance of time to spend with our children, or an abundance of opportunities for personal growth, gratitude for what *is* always opens us up to what *can be.* The more grateful we *are,* the more we attract to be grateful *for.* Manifesting abundance is not a secret; it is merely a matter of providing it with a home where it can thrive. Abundance prospers when gratitude provides a welcoming environment. It's the count-your-blessings principle in action. One blessing leads to another and another and another. This is a lavishly abundant universe, and absolutely all of its bounty is available to our good home.

The goal is to get our consciousness to that place where the glass half-empty or half-full dilemma is no longer even an issue because that glass is always overflowing its rim. When we find ourselves happily knee-deep in the river of overflowing abundance, it's a pretty good sign that we've created the perfect good home for spirit's limitless supply of treasures.

Health

Vibrant health is a free gift, but we have to value it if we want to continue to receive its benefits. We say that "if you have your health, you have everything," but we often seem to be experiencing *some*-thing less than health and vitality. Sometimes the "fix" is obvious and the only thing standing between us and the health we want is a willingness to put forth a little effort.

For example, even though I know that regular exercise and a healthy diet are good for my body, I still end up camping out in my den at least three days a week where my only "exercise" is pushing the chair away from the computer to get a new ream of paper or locate a stapler. I also find my car turning into my favorite fast food restaurant for a French fries fix at least once a month. (Factoring in some serious denial, the more realistic estimate is actually once or twice a week.) Then there are those little at-home indulgences. Running out of chocolate, for example, is tantamount to being taken off life support. Yet, through some strange process of rationalization and denial, I expect my body to operate optimally day in and day out, regardless of what I do or don't do to maintain it.

Of course, there's a great deal more to maintaining a healthy body than watching what we eat and how much we exercise. A good home for vibrant health is one that also understands the role of our thoughts, beliefs, and emotions in creating disease.

I struggled with airborne allergies most of my life. If it was a living thing, I was allergic to it. That's what I would tell people anytime they asked why my eyes were always red, my nose was constantly stuffed up, and why I had handkerchiefs to match every outfit. I sneezed my way through April, May, August, and September and recoiled in fear every time I walked into anyone's home who had live plants or shedding animals.

Then one day, a friend said something that changed my life. "Maybe you're not really allergic to *all* living things; maybe you're just allergic to one or two," he said. "Maybe it's *who* you're allergic to rather than *what*." I spent the next week journaling on my relationship with my mother. Within a month, my mother and I had made a major breakthrough and my allergies were reduced by at least seventy-five percent. Within two years, they disappeared entirely.

Our mental and emotional well-being can dictate when, how, and if illness manifests in our physical bodies. We all know the toll stress takes on us. We've been inundated with information about the mind-body connection. Providing a good home for perfect health is as much about what we're thinking and feeling, as it is what we're doing.

We value the free gift of a healthy physical body by providing it with the love and care it requires. Spending a little time each day expressing gratitude for the amazing way in which our body functions, day after day (often in spite of how we use and abuse it), will remind us of what an amazing gift it truly is and keep the door open for more and more good health to show up in our lives.

Job/Career/Work

If you want the universe to hook you up with your dream job, you need the courage to pursue what you love without compromise. That doesn't mean you quit working and wait for the job fairy to arrive at your door with an offer that allows you to pursue your passion at twice your current salary, three times the benefits, and four months of paid vacation a year. It *does* mean that you do what it takes to do what you love. That might involve additional schooling, trimming your budget, or moving to a new location (possibly outside your comfort zone).

It definitely means that you need to know what you want and why you want it. I fantasized about being a ballerina when I was eight. It took only three ballet lessons for me to realize hard work, sore muscles, and a wafer-thin-body were all job requirements. I was in love with the fantasy (and the fluffy pink tutus), not the career path. Reality checks are a good idea, and as for me, I was ready to check that job off my wish list by the time I was nine.

Finding your passion may take some inside work, and pursuing it may require unrelenting determination, but once you figure it out, your free gift of perfect employment will show up beautifully wrapped and custom-made to meet your greatest expectations.

Relationships

If our spiritual house is built on a foundation of love, good relationships come easily. Add a little gratitude for the people in your life and you're good to go. Nothing trumps love, compassion, and caring when it comes to attracting loving relationships into your life. If we make sure there aren't any "hazardous conditions" compromising the relationship, there's no limit to the amount of free love (more sustainable than the 60s variety) we can have.

It's all freely available—abundance, health, the right job, and loving relationships—as long as we have the consciousness to receive gifts and a good home large enough to accommodate them.

At the time we adopted Crystal for my daughter, there was a lot of space in our hearts, but very little in our physical house. Crystal soon became a furry fixture in virtually every room at some point in the day. Within a year, we manifested a larger living space, one that provided even roomier accommodations for Crystal, where she had both indoor and outdoor privileges and a grassy rabbit run in the back yard. With all that newfound space, Crystal effortlessly manifested a boy bunny buddy. His name was Biggles. No, we didn't find him at a garage sale, but it was definitely a déjà vu experience. We found him at the county fair where he was stretched out in a handmade hutch next to a sign that read, "Free to Good Home."

Proceed When Clear

I've been the butt of my kids' jokes for years. It's that natural progression in our relationship from doting parent/loving child to crazy old lady/ embarrassed offspring. Apparently, it's a cultural obligation to let the world see how wildly amusing your parents become after turning fifty.

Consequently, my children have had a few laughs at my expense. For example, son to friend: "Did you hear the one about how my mom ran into the bank . . . (wait for it) . . . literally? In my defense, I wasn't driving that fast—I was creeping along while rummaging through my purse for my deposit when suddenly that brick wall next to the drive-up window appeared out of nowhere, and the rest is family comedy history. The punch line: my insurance agent, apparently unconcerned about **my** wellbeing or that of my midlife crisis BMW, queried . . . (wait for it) . . . did you hurt the bank?

Of course, I had a few laughs at my mother's expense as well after she crossed over into seniorhood. For example: Me (laughing so hard I am almost drooling as I speak) to my friend: "Did I ever tell you about my mom's close encounter with a railroad crossing? It seems she tried to beat a train by speeding across the tracks, but came to an abrupt stop when the crossing arms came crashing down on the hood of her car? Oh, and then, in a panic, she threw the car in reverse, hit the gas and . . . (wait for it) . . . crashed into the car behind her."

No, it's not some early form of dementia that takes over sometime after age fifty—it's the delayed effects of years of living clueless—alternating between acts of impulse and acts of denial—as though we wore a cloak of invincibility that rendered us immune to disagreeable consequences.

Paying attention to what's happening around you (and inside you) before moving forward is one of those common sense recommendations that are uncommonly heeded until we're hopelessly lost and confused, and our families are checking out retirement homes for Mom "just in case."

We know that living our lives with reckless abandon is irresponsible at best and cataclysmic at worst, but we continue to stumble over our own directional signs.

When we learn to slow down, pay attention, and then proceed when clear . . . (wait for it) . . . it becomes clear how to proceed.

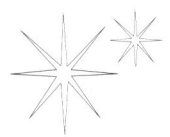
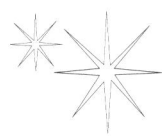

CHAPTER
14

I'm frequently guilty of leaping before looking, diving right in, jumping to conclusions, making a mountain out of a molehill, speaking before thinking, and all those other clichéd acts of impulse and insanity that get people into trouble.

My behavior is okay, I rationalize, because it is merely a reflection of my spirited personality, and if I act a little rashly at times, it's nothing to be concerned about. I do what works for me in the moment and deal with any fallout later.

As painful as it is to confess that my impulsive behavior hasn't always served me, I am willing to admit to an occasional "What did I *think* was going to happen?" misstep. My Good Judgment meter wasn't accurately calibrated, and what started out as a potentially magical impromptu journey down the yellow brick road often ended up being a nightmarish trip through the Coney Island of my mind. Yet, I kept following "detour signs" that took me through one roundabout after another and dropped me off at the wrong exit.

"The universe threw me a curve, and I have no idea why!" I would protest loudly. I didn't see it coming, I couldn't have possibly predicted *that* outcome, and life seems like a random number generator operated by a God that enjoys pushing buttons.

My mother was a lot like me, but Mom's lessons in course correction were learned mostly in her car. In spite of a lengthy list of everything from amusing to mind-boggling incidents with her vehicle over the years, at age seventy-nine, she still drove as though she was an indestructible sixteen-year-old . . . with an attitude. That's why the phone call I received from the local police that particular day didn't really surprise me. Apparently, Mom had sneaked out with her car only a few minutes after promising that she would spend the day at home working on a holiday craft project.

I knew she hadn't wanted to stay home; far more exciting options awaited beyond the front door of her house, she insisted. That may have been true, but I also knew that the bridge club meeting she wanted to attend meant a fifteen-mile drive on a heavily-traveled section of the interstate, and I had my concerns about her safety . . . *and* that of the hundreds of other drivers/passengers she was going to race past at ninety miles an hour. She told me I was exaggerating.

Not really. She was once stopped by a police officer (who followed her, lights flashing, for twenty miles before she noticed him in her rearview mirror) for doing ninety-five in a sixty-five mph zone. And if a speed-limits-be-damned mindset wasn't enough to warrant grounding, there was her growing list of medications—all of which carried dire warnings about operating any machine more sophisticated than a hand mixer—and continued problems with her vision. Her doctor backed me up, making it clear that even allowing her the occasional donut run to the King Soopers' supermarket two miles away would be a major concession.

So that day, my emotions ran the gamut from annoyance, to confusion, to panic when, less than an hour after my heart-to-heart with Mom, my purse suddenly came alive with the sound of music emanating from my cell phone. The caller ID screamed "police" and I took a deep breath before answering. The familiar female voice on the other end of the line struggled to maintain a light, funny-thing-just-happened tone, but I wasn't smiling. She was just "hunky dory," Mom insisted, but there had been a minor accident; her new Chevy was being towed to the repair shop, and she needed a ride home.

When I arrived fifteen minutes later, I encountered three police cars that had been called to the scene of this *minor* mishap, but there was no trace of Mom. After a short conversation with one of the officers, I spied Mom in the front seat of the tow truck, slumping down, avoiding my glance, and trying hard to become invisible.

Her explanation of what happened was creative, if not credible. She was simply turning left onto this deserted highway, she explained, when suddenly a speeding car appeared out of nowhere, ran her off the road, and then disappeared in a cloud of dust as quickly as it had come. The police officer's version was less colorful: in an attempt to make a left-hand turn onto a very congested highway, she had "gunned it" to force her way in. In doing so, she had over steered into the ditch on the other side of the road and come to a stop in six inches of mud. Regardless of the details of the incident, she was more shaken than she was willing to admit, but okay. The car hadn't fared as well. It was hitched to the tow truck and was ready to limp its way to the garage.

The drive home was painfully awkward. It was at least ten minutes before either of us said anything. Mom finally broke the silence with a sudden explosion of words fired in rapid succession—all in defense of her actions: "Yes, I know I said I would stay home, but I had a very invigorating surge of energy which I hated to waste, *and* spending time with my card group is so much more exciting than staying home making miniature Christmas trees out of pipe cleaners, *and* I took only the back roads where there was no traffic, *and* the car that almost hit me was driving way too fast, *and* if some busybody hadn't phoned the cops on me in the first place, I could have just called AAA and none of this fuss would have been necessary, *and* . . ."

Ah, the power of rationalization. She was doing such a good job of working its magic, that she almost had me convinced. The truth was that she acted on impulse without first thinking things through. Then she had the misfortune to get caught. It was an unfortunate gotcha! The end result wasn't pretty, yet I couldn't really be angry with her. I completely understood.

My own ability to step back, carefully consider my choices, and wait patiently for the right opportunity to act was somewhere around a minus two on a scale of one to ten—and that's what this entire incident was really about.

It was easy to confuse impulse with intuition. Every time the little light bulb went on in my head saying, "This looks like fun!" and my body responded with that electrifying tingle of excitement, I charged forward. If it looks *and* feels like a good idea, how could it be anything else?

Impulse is a powerful intoxicant. One minute, we're stuck in a boring place of "sameness," and the next minute, feeling a bit light-headed and giddy, we're responding to a sudden, delicious desire to do something spontaneous and new, to pay attention to impossible-to-ignore cues that are telling us to *go for it*. Impulse's appeal is that it gives us a power rush (however temporary it may be).

Intuition can also leave us feeling euphoric and powerful. However, intuition doesn't send us down a path that leads to the edge of a high cliff with a rushing river two hundred feet below.

Instead, intuition always sends us down the road to lifelong success and empowerment. How can we tell the difference between the two? By paying attention.

Mom's defense for the unfortunate ditch incident relied heavily on the presence of a "phantom" car that appeared out of "nowhere." Let's be honest: nothing appears out of nowhere. She just pulled out onto that crossroad without looking. If she'd taken the time to notice what was happening around her, the accident might not have happened. I recently encountered an intriguing sign at the Denver airport that read, *Proceed When Clear.* It was posted in a parking area where people are always rushing to get in their cars, through the exits, and on to their next destination—with minimal awareness of anybody or anything around them. The *Proceed When Clear* sign was a reminder to stay focused and attentive.

I began thinking about how this sign should be routinely posted at all intersections on all roads, nailed over the entrance of any shopping mall having a clearance sale, and glued to the foreheads of every teenager who owns (or uses) both a car and a not-a-smart-idea cell phone. It pretty much says it all: *Proceed When Clear.* All other signs suddenly become redundant. Operating a motor vehicle without fully focusing on what you're doing, where you're going, and what's about to run you over is just plain irresponsible. Living your life without following those same guidelines is even more reckless.

There are lots of ways to train ourselves to slow down and pay more attention to what's going on around us *and* within us; one of which is meditation. Meditation is the enemy of impulse.

It has been my experience that most impulsive people can't meditate. When I say "my experience," I mean it literally. Remaining still long enough to hear the voice within wasn't in my repertoire. The first time I was told to get comfortable in my chair, close my eyes, and move into the silence for twenty minutes, I had the beginnings of a panic attack. You want me to do what? Sit *still*!? And for *how* long? What if I get thirsty? What if I need to use the restroom? What if my foot falls asleep? What if I get to a point where I just can't sit still anymore and bolt for the door and everyone in the class starts thinking I'm unstable and they begin to talk behind my back and before I know it I'm shunned by everyone and banned from future classes and . . .

This meditation thing felt more like some sick form of torture than the first step on the path to a spiritual awakening. I flashed back to second grade when Mrs. Mean made me sit silently in the corner for an hour and contemplate what I'd done. What I'd done!? It was just gum and all Diane had to do to get it out of her hair was cut off her ponytail! What was I supposed to think about in that corner—*other* non-traditional ways to use gum? What I *did* think about was how many more days there were until summer vacation.

That's probably why the first words that formed in my head during that introductory meditation class were, "You're not the boss of me," followed by, "You can't make me."

After that first disastrous attempt at meditating, I made a pact with the instructor to go home and try just five minutes of meditation at first, and work up from there. Even five minutes felt like an eternity, but I'd made a promise.

I managed to survive two minutes of meditating at home before melting down. I decided that maybe it was the hard, straight-backed chair. But soft, cushy chairs were even worse—it took almost three minutes to just collapse the footrest on the twenty-year-old overstuffed recliner, making a quick, "emergency" exit nearly impossible.

I then tried changing up locations. Maybe a quieter, darker guest room would be a better place to meditate? Or a sunroom with thirty-four plants, a small pond, and seven fish? Or in the bedroom next to the nightstand with the King Tut table fountain on top? Or on the back deck under the patio umbrella? Or stretched out on top of the hot tub cover? Nothing worked. Why? Because I wasn't ready.

When I was a senior in college I had to take a World Religions class to fulfill my humanities requirement. I tried unsuccessfully to substitute some other course—*any* other course—but my counselor stood firm. It was a lecture class with a couple hundred students and one overworked professor. In addition to the hour-long lectures three times a week, we were also required to attend small evening discussion groups of ten to twelve students. The professor facilitated each group's first meeting himself and then assigned one of the group members to run the sessions for the rest of the semester.

After the first evening session, I received a note from the professor asking me to drop by his office for a chat. I couldn't imagine what he wanted; I'd been careful to remain as inconspicuous as possible, contributing only as much to the discussion that night as was necessary. Religion wasn't my thing, and my strategy was to simply survive the course with the absolute minimal effort required to get a B. Apparently, my plan hadn't worked. He'd somehow singled me out and was even requesting a meeting.

I'd heard the professor was a practicing Buddhist, and the appearance of his office seemed to confirm that assessment. There were only the barest of elements present—a desk, a desk chair, a stool for visitors, and a humble little bookcase. After inviting me to take a seat on the stool, he closed his eyes for a few moments and then opened them slowly, looking directly at me. "Linda," he said, "I would like to offer you the opportunity to lead your World Religions discussion group. I see a spiritual teacher in you. Teaching this class will put you on your path."

I reeled in horror. What? I stood up immediately and began listing the top three reasons why I couldn't take over the discussion group. One, I explained: I'm not a religion major, so this isn't my job. Two: I'm in the middle of rehearsals for *A Flea in Her Ear* and don't have time to take on anything else right now.

Three: The only teaching I saw in my future were theatre classes at some university as far away from downstate Illinois as possible. Thanks, but no thanks. Teaching religion or spirituality, or anything even remotely God-related, was definitely *not* on my list of things I planned to do with my life.

Not once during my entire temper tantrum did he take his eyes off me. He watched, somewhat bemused, as I frantically grabbed my books and headed for the door. When I turned back to say goodbye, he smiled at me and said, in a voice that I would now describe as eerily similar to Yoda's, "You can do this now, or you can do this later, but you will do it."

I walked away thinking this man had spent way too many years sitting in the lotus position contemplating the windowless walls in his office. If I'd taken even a few minutes to ask him a few questions about what he meant, or gone inside to tap my intuition for guidance, or even paid attention to the excited butterflies in my stomach hoping to be freed, I could have saved myself twenty years of wandering aimlessly trying to find my true calling.

Seeing ourselves from a higher perspective takes a conscious effort. Clarity can be a long, arduous process, and it begins by peeling away one layer of our protective outer covering (the ego) at a time.

It's like those brightly painted wooden Russian nesting dolls, where each opened container reveals yet another one tucked inside. Each new understanding about our self leads to more questions and more opportunities for even deeper insights. We don't even notice that the next doll *can* be opened until we've reached the next level of awareness. Getting to that smallest doll—the one tucked inside the one that's tucked inside the previous one, which is tucked inside the one before that . . ., and so on, is the gift of real clarity. Getting to that final "doll" isn't always easy. Some of those nesting sets come with more dolls-inside-of-dolls than others. We often don't know how many are in our particular set ahead of time. We also don't know exactly how long it will take to open them all. What we *do* know, however, is that when there are finally no more dolls to be opened, we're clear enough to proceed. The consequences of our actions start becoming less destructive and more empowering.

With each uncovered layer and each new discovery about ourselves, we learn a lot about what we most often fail to see coming and what is most likely to run us over. Maybe we're easily able to avoid those six-wheelers, but the mid-size sedans get us every time—especially the red ones. Knowing that, we can make the adjustments necessary to ensure that we never get tire-tracked again. We can pull out into "traffic" without getting broadsided by a metaphorical speeding truck. Instead, we effortlessly become part of the flow. Life begins to make a lot of sense and new realizations occur daily.

Getting clear requires a commitment to opening each and every one of those nesting dolls . . . in order . . . one at a time . . . at whatever pace is required . . . for as long as it takes to get to the last one. Spiritual practices, such as meditation, create the space we need to tap into the clarity and guidance we desire. There are many different forms of meditation and they don't all require sitting in a chair or anyplace else. Walking, gardening, spending time in nature, and journaling are only a few ways in which we can court spiritual awareness through meditation. Meditation hones our ability to hear (and have the courage to heed) the whispers of intuition.

Waiting to proceed until we are clear does not mean we should never take a chance or act spontaneously. If we are so immobilized by fear that we remain in *Park* all of our lives, we'll never even begin our journey, much less reach its destination. *Proceed When Clear* does not mean *STOP*; it merely means pay attention before trying to break the land speed record.

That way, when we *do* move forward, we know the *where* and the *why* of our journey. That's when choosing the "how" among an infinite number of glorious possibilities becomes the joyful adventure of a lifetime. If we *Proceed When Clear* . . . (wait for it) . . . we can fast forward to "the rest of our life" and secure a happy forever after when we get there.

Exit

It's important to recognize the difference between making an entrance and making an exit. Otherwise, you might never know for sure if you're coming or going.

One of the problems in distinguishing between an entrance and an exit is that one often leads to another, and it's easy to become confused during the transition.

It's a little like those crazy revolving doors. You push on one with the intent of entering some big city downtown department store, and before you know it, you're back on the street where you started, lost and confused. You've exited right past the entrance without even knowing it. Of course, you can try again, and as long as you keep pushing, you'll have repeated opportunities to enter and exit, enter and exit, enter and exit, again and again and again.

I usually got the hang of it within three or four revolutions, and somehow I managed to end up inside the store, breathing hard and feeling a little dizzy, but still euphoric at having reached my destination—the main entryway, about twenty feet from the perfume counter.

I faced the same challenge trying to leave. Only on the return trip, I was also juggling an armful of shopping bags and a to-go box from the fourth floor café. Catching an opening as the door spun round and round, and then jamming myself and all my packages into one of the impossibly small pie-shaped sections was a whole other level of challenge. It took at least two complete revolutions to rebalance my bags and another couple to successfully eject onto the sidewalk.

One day, after dropping my purse, dumping the contents of two shopping bags, and losing a shoe, a sales clerk pointed out the standard, open-step through-shut glass door off to the side. "I can use that door?!" I exclaimed, somewhat bewildered. That's really available to me? I thought those were only for folks in wheelchairs and firemen racing to the third floor smoking lounge.

How many turns of that revolving door had I suffered through over the years before I was open to seeing the simpler choice, the one that made entrances and exits both graceful and effortless?

Consider how many experiences we enter and exit during a lifetime, or a decade, a year, a month, a week, a day . . . even an hour. Life is one big entrance and exit with lots of smaller ones scattered throughout. We are beings in motion; we enter and exit all the time. We enter into contracts, relationships, stores, and businesses. We enter into structured learning experiences, i.e., elementary school, high school, college, etc., and unstructured ones. And most importantly, we enter onto "stages" of all kinds. One way or another, we also exit all of these same things. Every experience changes us in some way, with or without our permission.

Shakespeare said that "all the world's a stage, and all the men and women merely players: they have their exits and their entrances; and one man in his time plays many parts."

His famous words have not gone unnoticed; they've been immortalized on bumper stickers, posters, t-shirts, bookmarks, and just about anything else that can be marketed for $19.95 or less. Clichéd as it has become, it's still an important message.

We have roles to play as we enter and exit the different stages of our lives (birth is our entrance and death our exit), and we are always "on stage" performing for one audience or another, in one way or another.

It's important to have a "large stage" consciousness—an awareness that everything we do and think is part of our personal script—the one we continually edit with each new understanding. Mastering large stage consciousness makes graceful exits off the smaller stages in our lives easy and effortless.

Part of that learning process is to recognize when we're pushing into things, and when we've overstayed in a situation. And when it's time to make an exit, it's helpful to know exactly which exit is yours.

The Academy Awards are a good example. Every person who ends up on that stage is an experienced actor who knows a few things about entrances and exits. Or not. How many winners, upon completing their acceptance speech, look like Bambi in the headlights, absolutely clueless as to which way they need to go to get off the stage? Apparently, I'm not the only one who has noticed this strange phenomenon because there's always a stash of stunning starlets waiting in the wings to escort the confused actor to the appropriate exit.

Even more curious are the winners who don't seem to understand the concept of exits at all. Their brief acceptance speeches somehow morph into painfully long monologues that threaten to go on for hours. Clearly, they don't realize that there are consequences for not making a timely exit. They always seem slightly startled when, after having exceeded the allotted time by a factor of ten, the orchestra pumps up the volume and slowly, but surely, drowns them out. If that doesn't work (and it often doesn't), they pull out all the stops and go to a commercial break.

It's important to know when you're done with something . . . or it's done with you.

And then . . . exit stage right (or left) with your dignity, integrity, and self-respect still intact.

Part of the difficulty is that exits can be more difficult to find than entrances. Maybe that's why it always seems easier to get into things than out of them. For example, no one ever complained that it was hard to get into trouble. Getting out of it? Well, that's a whole different story.

Finding an exit on short notice can be especially tricky, particularly in the dark (which we often are at those critical moments). There's a reason they light up exit signs. I've seen very few entrance signs lit up. There's no need for it. Entrances are everywhere. The universe offers us so many options—a world of infinite possibility—so many doors to try, so many experiences to explore. But no one ever said we had to explore all of them. Some things are meant for us and some are not.

Once we become entangled in an experience, however, even if it's glaringly obvious to everyone we know that we're hopelessly lost, it's a real challenge to gain the perspective we need to even begin looking for an exit, much less finding one. We just keep "dancing," oblivious to what else is going on around us, long after we should have demanded that someone bring down the curtain.

If we fail to make a timely exit, chances are there's a Hook out there somewhere with our name on it. And it may show up as heartache, a job loss, a series of financial disasters, and so on.

There are less painful ways to end an experience. They're called exit strategies. The term comes from the world of business, but it's one of those common sense ideas with lots of practical applications.

Exit strategies typically answer the question: What if? What if this doesn't work out the way I'm envisioning it? What if my path leads me in a different direction? Will I be able to exit this situation gracefully and without regrets? Will I exit to a standing ovation or be pummeled with rotten tomatoes?

I have lots of divorced friends who are still picking tomato seeds out of their hair. Relationships, possibly more than anything else in our lives, need exit strategies. All too often, they begin with marginally delusional expectations, and end with more devastation than a natural disaster.

That was certainly my experience. The script I bought into for my first marriage went something like this: After the introductory opening scene (the proposal), the handsome prince marries the lovely maiden. They have even lovelier children, and the prince vows to take care of her (and the kids) for the rest of their lives. Bluebirds perch on her windowsill every morning and sing happy tunes, forest friends take care of the housekeeping, and gaily dressed gnomes with pointed hats handle the finances.

The handsome prince returns home from work every evening with freshly picked roses (thorns removed), handles meal preparation while the maiden naps, and massages her feet before she retires for the evening. Why would anyone need an exit strategy from a story like that?

I knew better than to really believe that, of course. I'd known better since I was about six, when I learned to read and discovered my mother had been sanitizing my bedtime stories by skipping over the "grim" in the Grimm's Fairy Tales. That was probably why it always seemed odd to me that Snow White suddenly developed an allergy to fruit . . . but was able to sleep it off.

It was easier for me to buy into an idealized future than to invest a lot of time working on my low self-worth and lack of problem solving skills. I stayed in a marriage that wasn't working for way too many years because I didn't have an exit strategy and implementing one retroactively is a lot like that old adage about closing the barn door after the horse has run away—too little, and way, way too late. I stayed longer than I should have because I didn't know how to be independent, I wasn't in a position to be able to support three children by myself, and I had absolutely nowhere to go.

When I finally made my exit in about the clumsiest way possible, there was no applause. A couple of weak attempts at an encore didn't work any better and, in fact, I was greeted with loud, prolonged booing, led by the people who cared for me most.

Finding a way to extricate yourself from an unempowering situation is not easy. But it helps if you're open to all possibilities. Sometimes you have to find a creative way to exit a situation, but you DO have to exit. It also helps if you can maintain a sense of humor during the process.

Exits are always available if you're willing to look for them. Rarely can you go out the same door you came in. You've changed, you've grown, you're not in the same place you were when you began, and that original entrance is not available to you anymore.

I think it's interesting that sometimes in business, exit strategies are called, "Harvest Strategies." I love that! It makes sense in any situation to do everything we can to ensure the most bountiful harvest possible and then move on to something new.

Spiritually, an exit strategy is about a growth in consciousness. It's not a worst case scenario plan; it's a commitment to taking good care of ourselves and making conscious choices. It's asking the right questions and listening to the answers.

What lessons does this experience have for me? How can I honor and respect other people who may also be involved? Am I prepared to find the "gift" in this experience, regardless of the outcome?

With an exit strategy in place, both entrances and exits become effortless. No more closed doors, no more Hooks, no more badly scripted dramas. No more revolving doors.

We get to choose the when and how of all our exits. We get to squeeze the juice out of every experience and when we're satiated, we get to say, "that's all, folks" in whatever way works for us. We get to take a bow, bring down the curtain, and exit stage right. And we get to say, THE END.

Acknowledgments

Please Pass the Crayons

There is no more humbling an experience than writing a book. It's a little like being handed one of those crazy-large boxes of crayons with 120 colors—some of which have mystifying names like Mango Tango, Fuzzy Wuzzy, and Neon Carrot—and being told you're expected to do something magical (and, of course, marketable) with them. Most of these colors weren't even yet a twinkle in the eye of the Crayola Company when I was a child; the most exotic shade I was asked to create with was Burnt Sienna, and no one seemed to notice anyway if I opted for basic brown. Yet, you have this nagging feeling that unless you at least experiment with all 120, you might miss out on a life-defining new shade, tint, or hue that could make the difference between senseless scribble and mind-expanding masterpiece.

Finally, several years later, the crayon box is empty, the sticks of colors have been worn down to a waxy nub, and the project is complete. And maybe, just maybe, you have a masterpiece worthy of a refrigerator and a magnet.

Anyone who ever uttered those fateful words, "I want to be a writer when I grow up!" knows that the authoring experience is a lot of late nights, early mornings, and failed attempts to run away from home. It's also exhilarating, exciting, and, dare I say it, joyous fun. My journey of over 3,000 days was not completed alone. Mentors, friends, and team members showed up to assist whenever I needed them, right on cue.

They sharpened my crayons when they had clearly lost their point and encouraged me to explore Cosmic Cobalt even when I insisted that I was *not* interested in exploring the blues. They listened patiently to my mystifying out-loud "thought processing" and never even batted an eye when I announced I was trying to find a way to work on my laptop in the hot tub. They were a sign from God in the form of the support team from heaven. They kept funding more and more boxes of crayons, never asking what happened to the previous sets.

With that in mind, I'd like to dedicate the most important colors in my Crayola box to the following Team-Linda members:

Purple Mountains Majesty—*Bob Potter*: I *so* appreciate my husband who cheerfully accompanies me on all my crazy-steep, uphill climbs. This one was a doozey.

Rose Quartz—*Dawn Murray*: A beautiful gem of a daughter, generous with her compliments and thoughtful with her critiques. She handled me so gently, I didn't even mind the occasional, "Mom, get a grip."

Atomic Tangerine—*Nicole Kelly*: My multi-talented daughter (and fellow writer) who kept my feet to the fire while I had my head in the clouds. Somehow it worked.

Wild Blue Yonder—*Derek Abbott*: My "rocket-scientist" son graciously allowed me to tell embarrassing childhood stories about him in the name of "literature." (Even the one about his Superman Underoos...)

Wild Watermelon—*Aidan Murray*: There is no sweeter, joy-filled inspiration than grandchildren. They are the seeds of a happy-ever-after.

Macaroni and Cheese—*Grandpuppies* (*Bella, Kobe, Macintosh and Madison*). When the going gets a little tough, dog kisses are even better than comfort food. Need I say more?

Basic Green—*Rev. John Pons*: John helped me see the forest for the trees. It's nice to have someone with a greater grasp of the big picture with you at the beginning of a life-defining journey.

Off Road—*Fred Knight*: It's a true gift to have a friend who can help you discern when the road less traveled is the empowering choice, and when it's simply a weed infested mine field.

Blast off Bronze—*Donna Visocky*. The most fearless person I know, *boldly going where no woman has gone before*. It took her three years to finally convince me it was my time to launch.

White with Confetti Glitter—*Whole Life Center for Spiritual Living*. Never underestimate the value of cheerleaders. I've had an entire spiritual community full of them for over 15 years. Team-Linda says thanks!

Piggy Pink—*The Hamm Family*: I once had a t-shirt that said, "Once a Hamm, always a ham." My ham family is an endless source of wildly entertaining memories.

Magic Potion—*Toni D. Holm, Publisher*: It's a true gift to be able to transform a manuscript with multiple personality disorder (by a first-time author) into a book with a message in its madness.

Razzle Dazzle Rose—*John and Kate-Romero Stellar (Stellar Communications)*: It's a joy to have publicists who believe in your book's message as much as you do, and who know how to infuse just enough "Hollywood" to make it sparkle.

Lemon Lime Zing—*George E. Tice, Managing Editor*: He helped put the bomp in the bomp bah bomp bah bomp. Somebody had to. Thank you!

Pixie Powder: *Alece Birnbach, Cover Illustrator.* She not only captured the essence of the book, she sprinkled in a generous amount of whimsy.

Mixed Veggies—*The Production Staff*: Rose Kernan, RPK Editorial Services; Interior Design, Fleur de Lis Design; Pamela Ehn, copy editor, and Martha McMaster, proofreader. I'm grateful to have had a talented, caring staff managing the health of the book.

Thank God for every one of you!

About the Author

Linda M. Potter

Stand-up comedy was Ms. Potter's first career choice. Comedy, dry yet quirky with a PG-13 rating, is her natural calling. Practicality won out, though, and Potter pursued a BA degree in Speech and Theatre, and an MA degree in Theatre Arts. *BellaSpark Magazine* hired Ms. Potter as the magazine's Managing Editor, interviewing and writing feature articles on leading authors in body, mind, and spirit books, such as: Alan Cohen, Wayne Dyer, Deepak Chopra, Shirley MacLaine, Gregg Braden, John Randolph Price, Iyanla Vanzant, Lynn McTaggart, Joan Borysenko, Brian Weiss, James Twyman, John Holland, and Dr. Joe Dispenza. "I felt like a kid in a spiritual candy store!"

Potter's loyal readers loved the digestible, comedic insights offered in her quirky, yet grounded articles on life's challenges. Linda's spiritual armchair humor on *how to* ask for and recognize 'signs from God' caused her to be coined the *Erma Bombeck of Metaphysics*. Naturally, this lead to the writing of her book, *If Only God Would Give Me a Sign!* Where does Linda find her 'signs from God?' Signs are everywhere. They show up in the laundry room, outside her living room window, at the movies, art museums, airports, highways, shopping malls, or occasionally along a walking trail in the Rocky Mountain high country. You can reach Linda at www.lindampotter.com or www.wordkeepersinc.com.

Letter to the Reader

Dear Reader,

A guy at a party once asked me how I came up with all the crazy stories I tell. Before I could answer, he started gushing about the wildly creative, vivid imagination I must have. I didn't know what to say. Did he really think I made up the anecdotes I shared in my writing? "All those things really happened!" I blurted out. "Trust me, you can't make this stuff up!"

Is every detail in my stories absolutely accurate? That question assumes I actually **remember** every detail. My defense is that I'm over 60 and lucky I remember where I live (most of the time) much less every word of a conversation that took place in 1978. When I started writing about signs several years ago, I made a commitment to tell the truth and do my best ... and then fill in the blanks with my best guess. That's ok, I reasoned—most of the people I write about are as old as I am and they probably don't remember every detail either. This is a my-life-as-I-remember-it book, not a documentary. I do admit to intentionally changing names and a few telltale details here and there to protect the privacy of friends who might otherwise heave bricks through my front room window once the stories went public.

I wasn't as protective with family members—no fictionalized names there to protect the "guilty," just the whole stranger-than-fiction truth and all the consequences. Even the family dogs weren't spared full exposure. I'm sure they'll understand.

Of course, it's always important to be as honest as possible in everything we do, particularly with ourselves. We can't change what we don't see, and if we don't see what we need to change, we'll continue wandering down the path to nowhere in particular.

Searching for signs has been a great way for me to stay on track and keep the conversations with my Higher Self lively, entertaining, and *always* interesting. If, as you read this book, you resonate with my experiences, I invite you to take a closer look at your own. I suspect there are some life-lessons-in-common to be uncovered.

I've had lots of fun jotting down signs; they keep me aware and present as I go about my daily life. I've also enjoyed playing my Secret Signs game at talks and workshops. The game involves passing out sealed envelopes with pictures of different signs inside and having participants respond to what they get. It's interesting how everyone always seems to get the "right" envelope with the sign meant just for them.

Occasionally, I've had to remind people that this is just a game; that signs are food for thought, not omens or psychic readings.

After one of my workshops, a woman approached me with a question about the sign she received in her envelope. It was a yellow tornado warning sign that pictured a stick figure running from a swirling funnel cloud. Clearly concerned, she asked, "Does this mean that God is going to smite me with a tornado?" "Goodness, no!" I exclaimed. "Well, then, what does it mean?" she insisted. "That's for you to discover," I said, "but give yourself time to think about it." I explained that she would know when she'd found the answer, and I was betting it wouldn't involve any destructive twists. For now, I suggested, she could start by being grateful her name wasn't Dorothy and we weren't in Kansas. (My attempt to lighten the mood was *not* appreciated.) Undeterred, I pointed out that the running figure on the sign, while clearly frightened, was managing to stay well ahead of the storm.

She scowled at me a little and then returned to her seat, crumpling the sign paper between her fingers. A few minutes later she approached me again. This time she was smiling broadly. "I thought about it," she said, "and I've figured it out." "Well, what did you come up with?" I asked, taking the bait. "This sign was really meant for my twin sister. People get us mixed up all the time. (*Short, dramatic pause as she looked me straight in the eye before adding*....) I'd like a different one."

Signs are conversation starters. That conversation can be with your personal journal while snuggled up on the couch, with your higher self during a leisurely afternoon walk, with an old friend over a vanilla latte, or in any other scenario that feels comfortable.

Take a couple of intriguing signs to a lunch gathering or your book club meeting and see where the conversation goes. Chances are the signs will trigger a lively discussion. Things can be as light or as serious as the group desires. If you don't want to talk about *Dead End* or *No Public Restrooms* on that particular day, try inviting people to share a synchronistic experience they had over the past week and see what happens.

Most of all, I want you to just enjoy this book. I hope it makes you laugh. I hope it helps you cultivate a joy-filled relationship with your Spiritual source. I hope it encourages you to use the "God" word in public without feeling like you have to whisper. I hope it helps you *enlighten* up. I hope it opens the door to a fabulous life that celebrates the incredible, perfectly marvelous being you truly are.

Let me know how things go. I'd love to hear stories about your encounters with signs. I'd also love to hear about "ah-ha" moments—both little and large. Please visit my website where you'll find contact information, and the latest updates on my own *signs* journey. If you belong to a book club that selects *If Only God Would Give Me a Sign!*, I'd welcome the opportunity to speak with your group before or after you read it. If you do not belong to a book club, but would like to connect with me, I'd be honored. You may reach me at lindampotter@wordkeepersinc.com or www.lindampotter.com. Thank you for allowing me to share my personal, *true* experiences. I hope it was as deliciously fun for you as it was for me!

Linda M. Potter